DOCTOR JOHNSON
& Mr BOSWELL

SAMUEL JOHNSON, THE GREAT BEAR

From a photograph by Emery Walker, after the painting by James Barry, about 1781

PR3533.S17 ST. JOSEPH'S UNIVERSITY STX
Dr. Johnson & Mr. Boswell,
RELEASE
3 9353 00024 3665

Dr JOHNSON

& Mr BOSWELL

BY

HARRY SALPETER

89541 PR 3533 .S17

New York:

Coward-McCann, Publishers

1929

Copyright, 1929, by
Coward-McCann, Inc.
All rights reserved

Printed in the United States of America

TO

A. EDWARD NEWTON

BECAUSE HE, MORE THAN

ANY OTHER AMERICAN

HAS POPULARIZED

SAMUEL JOHNSON

& HIS GREAT BIOGRAPHER

CONTENTS

Contents

LIST OF ILLUSTRATIONS

List of Illustrations

CHAPTER ONE

"James Boswell met Samuel Johnson . . ."

Dr JOHNSON &

Mr BOSWELL

JAMES BOSWELL met Samuel Johnson for the first time on Monday, the 16th of May, 1763, in the back-parlour of the bookseller's shop of Mr. Thomas Davies, the actor. Sir Joshua Reynolds, who has projected the images of the chief figures of the Johnsonian age and bequeathed to us several illustrations for the Boswellian chronicle, neglected to give us a pictorial presentment of this superficially commonplace meeting at No. 8 Russell Street, Covent Garden. What of the extraordinary was there in a Boswell soliciting, and obtaining, an introduction to a Johnson? Boswell always was soliciting introductions and putting himself in the way and under the notice of celebrities. Johnson, formerly one of the wretched ones of Grub

Street (I refer to the condition, not the thoroughfare, which, if he trod at all, he trod only late in life) but now the oracle of literature, the court of appeals of morality, a pensioner of the Crown; Johnson, the Dictionary-maker, the English equivalent for the entire French Academy, was quite accustomed to being sought out and courted. Years ago he had felt strong enough to deny a dedication to, and reject the patronage of, the great Lord Chesterfield. But who can tell, at the moment of the event, where the commemoration tablet is to be placed, what scene, poem or painting shall celebrate? Only Boswell had a realization of the importance of this meeting, for himself, if not prescience of its significance for literary history. Let us then, with the indispensable help of Boswell's own recollection—and how many have not been obliged to that recollection and that assiduity—attempt to recapture that scene.

James Boswell, Esq., heir to the Scottish Laird of Auchinleck, a descendant through his great-grandfather, Alexander, Earl of Kincardine, of Robert Bruce; a young gentleman of twenty-two strongly inclined toward service in the Guards but compelled, by the edict of a stronger-willed father, in the direction of the law, and with a predilection for that kind of gaiety which included women and drink, although it did not exclude intelligent conversation—this young man was on Monday, May 16, 1763, in a considerable state of agitation. Ever since he had read Johnson's sturdy essays, and certainly after the publication of the great Dictionary, he had held the name of Samuel Johnson in something like veneration. Back in Scotland, eight months before, he had upheld the claims of the author of "The Rambler" against such doughty opposition as that furnished by Lord Kames, Adam Smith and others. Johnson happened to be the greatest living literary man in London, sufficient reason for Boswell desiring to meet him. That the impulse behind this desire was more deeply rooted than a celebrity hunter's one could not then know. Johnson was then fifty-four years of age, old enough to be Boswell's father and, in manners, a bear and not even a dancing bear. Provincial to his core, he had no great relish for Scotchmen, —pretending, possibly, a greater dislike than he felt—and Boswell was a Scotchman. In his Dictionary he had linked horses and Scotchmen as fellow-consumers of oats. [" Very true," replied Lord Elibank, " and where will you find such *men* and such *horses?"*] One can imagine Boswell's trepidation that day—if we picture, in the present, a young colonial-minded American who already had met all the Englishmen of social and literary distinction about to be ushered into the presence of the greatest English man of letters of his day, one, who, moreover, was known to be capable of rudeness to the point of cruelty and had also a strong distaste for Americans; especially for the literary sight-seeing type of American.

" Though then but two-and-twenty, I had for several years read his works with delight and instruction, and had the highest reverence for their authour, which had grown up in my fancy into a kind of mysterious veneration, by figuring to myself a state of solemn elevated abstraction, in which I supposed him to live in the immense metropolis of London." Ever since his first visit to that immense metropolis, three years before, in 1760, young Boswell had sought to obtain an audience with the great Cham of literature. At that time "Mr. Derrick the poet . . . flattered me with hopes that he would introduce me to Johnson, an honour of which I was very ambitious. But he never found an opportunity." In the summer of the following year Thomas Sheridan, father of the dramatist Richard Brinsley Sheridan, (who was then only ten years of age) was delivering lectures "upon the English Language and Publick Speaking to large and respectable audiences" in Edinburgh and Boswell heard him "frequently expatiate upon Johnson's extraordinary knowledge, talents and virtues, repeat his pointed sayings, describe his particularities, and boast of his being his guest sometimes till two or three in the morning." It was at this period that Boswell dropped so much money at the gaming table that he was obliged to borrow from his elocution teacher.

But upon returning to London at the end of the following year, he found that "an irreconcileable difference had taken place between Johnson and Sheridan." The latter, having been granted a pension of 200 pounds a year, since he held the actor's profession in low esteem, was moved to remark: "What! have they given *him* a pension? Then it is time for me to give up mine." Thus, Sheridan could not serve Boswell's purpose and the young Scotchman was compelled to return to his native heath, where, even in Edinburgh, he often felt like a Newmarket courser yoked to a dung-cart, as he wrote to his clerical friend, William Johnson Temple, the recipient of an amazing series of self-revelatory letters, so amazing that, by themselves, they put their author in the Pepysian class. In Edinburgh then, as later, Boswell alternated drunkenness with sobriety, lechery with contrition, convivial companionship with melancholy reflection and study.

Boswell paid his third visit to London in 1763, the desire to meet Johnson probably growing by denial and feeding in all likelihood upon the reports of those who had been favored with his conversation, or were acquainted with Johnsonian anecdotes. From David Hume, for example, Boswell had learned of Johnson's dislike for that philosopher, and of how he once left a room upon Hume entering it. In London Boswell presented himself to Mr. Davies with an introduction from Sheridan. Though of the stage, both Mr. and Mrs. Davies "maintained an uniform decency of character." She was beautiful and he "was a man of good understanding and talents, with the advantage of a liberal education" and with literary pretensions.

Much as he despised or affected to despise those who were, or had been, of the acting profession, Johnson could visit the Davieses without violence to his moral prejudices and Mr. Davies assured Mr. Boswell that in his shop circumstances might be propitious. Blessed with a mimic sense and a good memory, Davies recollected some of Johnson's sayings and imitated his voice and manner in such wise that "he increased my impatience more and more to see the extraordinary man whose works I highly valued, and whose conversation was reported to be so peculiarly excellent." Mimickry was an art which Boswell himself had practiced, abandoning it when he discovered that thus he provoked enmity. Davies was the man whom Charles Churchill, the great satiric poet of the day, was reported to have driven from the stage with his line in "The Rosciad:" "He mouths a sentence as curs mouthe a bone." He was later to become a bankrupt bookseller and Johnson was to dig into his own pockets and solicit funds to help him who was esteemed too much of a gentleman to succeed in any trade.

We can imagine Boswell calling on the Davieses more than once, calling at hours suggested by Mr. Davies as favorable to a meeting. No appointment seems to have been made, in deference, probably, to Boswell's fear that it might not be granted to one so obscure as himself. We must remember that although he had already met the great of Edinburgh, been patronized by the Earl of Eglinton, by him made a member of the Jockey Club at Newmarket, and had fawned upon the Duke of York, he had not yet gone forth upon his great tour of Europe, nor conducted his pertinacious sieges of Rousseau and Voltaire, nor puffed up the bladder of his vanity by presenting himself to Europe as the literary advocate of the struggling Corsicans. We can imagine Boswell calling several times, sitting in the back-parlour, nervously sipping tea, as he was doing on that memorable afternoon, and looking with a mixture of fear and expectation through the glass door every time a step is heard or a figure is seen entering from the street.

Verbal description and mimickry of the man, illustrated by Reynolds's painting of him after the publication of the Dictionary, must have made the person of Johnson familiar to Boswell before it was seen, as Boswell has made familiar to posterity the figure he came to know so well. And we can imagine his parting from the Davieses, after one of his futile waits, with some expression of disappointment on his side, and of assurance, on Davies's, and, in return, a promise to call again. He went off, perhaps to a tavern, or to some lady of easy virtue, or if it was the time for it, to a hanging at Tyburn for which kind of entertainment he had a morbid failing.

That no appointment was made, that Boswell called several times before the much-desired audience was granted are to be deduced from the three words in the following which I have italicized: "*At last,* on Monday, the 16th of May, when I was sitting in Mr. Davies's back-parlour, after having drunk tea with him and Mrs. Davies, Johnson *unexpectedly* came into the shop." It was Davies who saw him first through the glass door. Johnson probably was familiar with Davies's stock, or else darkness was descending, for contrary to his habit when among a collection of books, he did not pause but came "advancing towards us." It is likely that Johnson preferred to cast his good eye on Davies's wife rather than on his folios. ["That Davies hath a very pretty wife," wrote Churchill in the aforementioned "Rosciad".] Subsequently, when recalling the circumstances of this scene, Boswell must have perceived the humor lurking within this, to him, most serious of events, for he wrote—"he [Davies] announced his aweful approach to me, somewhat in the manner of an actor in the part of Horatio, when

SCENE OF THE FIRST MEETING

The bookshop of Thomas Davies, where Boswell first met Johnson. From a drawing by Hanslip Fletcher

he addresses Hamlet on the appearance of his father's ghost, 'Look, my Lord, it comes.'"

Enter Johnson, scrofula-marked, with his rolling gait, his twitching face, his brown coat spotted, his wig perhaps a little dirty and awry, his impressive bulk being sufficient to put the figure of the young Boswell in partial eclipse.

"I found that I had a very perfect idea of Johnson's figure." If it is a warm day and the back-parlour is not well-ventilated—which is altogether likely—the plump Boswell is perspiring and finding it hard to conceal the state of agitation in which he is. (He was of an excitable disposition.) "Mr. Davies mentioned my name, and respectfully introduced me to him," thus earning for ever a place in the history of English letters . . . "I was much agitated; and recollecting his prejudice against the Scotch of which I had heard much, I said to Davies, 'Don't tell where I come from.'—'From Scotland,' cried Davies roguishly." Boswell is all contrition. Davies earns a glance of pathetic reproof. He will explain that he cannot help his origin. "'Mr. Johnson, (said I,) I do indeed come from Scotland, but I cannot help it.' I am willing to flatter myself that I meant this as light pleasantry to sooth and conciliate him, and not as an humiliating abasement at the expence of my country. But however that might be, this speech was somewhat unlucky; for with that quickness of wit for which he was so remarkable, he seized the expression 'come from Scotland,' which I used in the sense of being of that country; and, as if I had said I had come away from it, or left it, retorted, 'That, Sir, I find is what a very great many of your countrymen cannot help.' This stroke stunned me a great deal; and when we had sat down I felt myself not a little embarrassed, and apprehensive of what might come next."

What came next was an underscoring of that rebuff. And had Boswell not been Boswell—had he suffered from a fine strain of sensitivity—English literature would have been the poorer by at least one great book and several great but insufficiently communicated personalities, insufficiently communicated in the sense that although others sent the message, it is Boswell's version that most of us have received and read. Much depends on the young man from the North as he stands in that back parlour cogitating what word or phrase he shall seize as his cue to return to notice and retrieve his embarrassed status.

Johnson has turned to Davies and is complaining of Garrick, who used to be his pupil and with whom he had come to London in 1737, Johnson to seek his fortune, Garrick to take up the study of law. Garrick, now at the height of fame, manager of Drury Lane, has refused to give Johnson a pass for Mrs. Williams, blind pensioner of Johnson's, a member of that unhappy and unruly flock to whom Johnson so generously provided shelter. Garrick has refused this pass, as Johnson puts it to Davies, "because he knows that the house will be full and that an order would be worth three shillings." [In January of 1756 Garrick had given a performance for the benefit of Mrs. Williams, which had brought her the sum of 200 pounds, so that Johnson's imputation against Garrick sounds somewhat perverse.] Re-enter Boswell, not then knowing, as he was later to discover, that "Johnson considered Garrick to be as it were his *property*," that no matter how roundly he himself berated Garrick, he would permit no one else to do so. "Eager to take any opening to get into conversation with him, I ventured to say, 'O, Sir, I cannot think Mr. Garrick would grudge such a trifle to you.' 'Sir, (said he, with a stern look,) I have known David Garrick longer than you have done: and I know no right you have to talk to me on the subject.' Perhaps I deserved this check: for it was rather presumptious in me, an entire stranger, to express any doubt of the justice of his animadversion upon his old acquaintance and pupil."

To poor Boswell all looked black. "I now felt myself much mortified and began to think that the hope which I had long indulged of obtaining his acquaintance was blasted." It was not until later that Boswell learned how easily Johnson gave rebuffs; what hurts, perhaps unknowingly, he inflicted upon men of thinner hides—although Boswell's was of an intermediate thickness—in his desire for victory in talk. Only twice after their intimacy had begun did

Johnson's rudeness hurt Boswell more—and on one of these occasions he remained away a week, being restored to good humor by Johnson's expression of regret. By what imponderable sums would we have been the poorer had Boswell, on that fateful May day, succumbed to the surface inevitability of events and given Johnson up forever—to that comparative obscurity which has swallowed men who have wielded even stronger pens, an obscurity from which not even all his writings combined with the industry of his pre-Boswell biographers would have saved him.

But "had not my ardour been uncommonly strong, and my resolution uncommonly persevering, so rough a reception might have deterred me for ever from making any further attempts. Fortunately, however, I remained upon the field not wholly discomfited, and was soon rewarded by hearing some of his conversation," of which he proceeds to give us a specimen. They had been left alone for part of the evening and Boswell "had ventured to make an observation now and then, which he received very civilly; so that I was satisfied that though there was a roughness in his manner, there was no ill-nature in his disposition," an important distinction and a vital one for the continuance of social intercourse with Johnson. For no man inflicted wounds so clean or bore less malice against the defeated once his victory was acknowledged. Even Walpole, one of his most bitter antagonists, marked that although Johnson was "very ill-natured at top," "he was good-natured at bottom." Regretfully, Boswell went off to keep another engagement, for he could not have known, when it was made, that he would meet Johnson that day, although it is rather surprising that the young Scotchman should have been punctilious enough to break away from Johnson in order to keep it. And when he parted, complaining to Davies of "the hard blows which the great man had given me, he kindly took upon him to console me by saying, 'Don't be uneasy. I can see he likes you very well.'" If Boswell believed Davies he went off to his engagement on wings.

Some days passed before Boswell made his first call on Johnson at his chambers, on the first floor of No. 1 Inner Temple Lane. But first he called on Davies and asked, in effect: Do you think I may call on Johnson? Might he not be annoyed? On the contrary, said Davies, "Mr. Johnson would take it as a compliment." "So upon Tuesday, the 24th of May, . . . I boldly repaired to Johnson," who received him "very courteously." Boswell then gives us his first description of Johnson, his apartment, his furniture, his dress, all of which were "sufficiently uncouth." "His brown suit of cloathes looked very rusty; he had on a little old shrivelled unpowdered wig, which was too small for his head; his shirt-neck and knees of his breeches were loose; his black worsted stockings ill drawn up; and he had a pair of unbuckled shoes by way of slippers." But once launched on talk, even on that first visit, "all these slovenly particularities were forgotten," a forgetfulness into which Johnson's talk could lull many of his generation. Boswell was soon to have his first token of Johnsonian favor. As was his custom, Johnson was conducting a levee and when some other gentlemen who had been in the room rose and left, Boswell thought it proper to follow their example and got up, probably expressing in some way a disinclination to leave. And Johnson said: "'Nay, don't go.' 'Sir, (said I) I am afraid that I intrude upon you. It is benevolent to allow me to sit and hear you.' He seemed pleased with this compliment, which I sincerely paid him, and answered, 'Sir, I am obliged to any man who visits me.'" And then follows another 'minute' of Johnson's talk. "And when I rose a second time he again pressed me to stay, which I did." The Johnson-Boswell alliance is in the process of being cemented.

Johnson told Boswell of his schedule, "that he generally went abroad at four in the afternoon, and seldom came home till two in the morning." Boswell even elicited the admission from Johnson that "it was a bad habit" and the younger man, years later on putting together his notes and recalling his intimated reproof, marvels at his daring and that Johnson "bore it with so much indulgence." Before they parted, Johnson promised to visit Boswell at his lodgings and "as I took my leave, shook me cordially by the hand." When we bear in mind Johnson's fear of solitude and his derivatory love of company and of talk, when we consider in what an attitude of humble veneration Boswell placed himself and how pleasing to an old man—especially to a lone and childless old man—must be the tokens of a younger man's admiration, when we recall that Boswell, from the beginning, showed no inclination to cross, or contest, or chivy, him, but, rather, was prepared to feed him cues for victorious talk—then, from this point onward, we see that no hammer can sever the links binding Boswell to Johnson. Reporting the conclusion of this first visit, Boswell writes: "It is almost needless to add that I felt no little elation at having now so happily established an acquaintance of which I had been so long ambitious."

"My readers will, I trust," he continues, "excuse me for being thus minutely circumstantial, when it is considered that the acquaintance of Dr. Johnson was to me a most valuable acquisition, and laid the foundation for whatever instruction and entertainment they may receive from my collections concerning the great subject of the work which they are now perusing."

Johnson was visited again on Monday, June 13th, and, at parting, "asked me why I did not come oftener to him." Boswell recalled the severity of Johnson's manner at Davies's book shop and Johnson pooh-poohed it away. They met again near Temple Bar several days later, at 1 in the morning, but it was too late for a swig at the tavern, and they did not meet again until Saturday, June 25, and then quite by accident "at Clifton's eating-house, in Butcher-row," where, unobserved, Boswell overheard Johnson engage in a dispute with an Irish gentleman "concerning the cause of some part of mankind being black." The argument grew so hot that Johnson walked away (this is probably the only instance of Johnson's evasion of an adversary), Boswell, still unobserved, following him.

They agreed to meet that evening at the Mitre Tavern, No. 39 Fleet Street, the favorite among Johnson's taverns. They had port wine and Boswell felt "a variety of sensations and a pleasing elevation of mind beyond what I had ever before experienced," his state being induced by the sound of the tavern's High Church name, delight in being seen in Johnson's company on familiar terms and "the extraordinary power and precision of his conversation." During that evening, Boswell, finding the occasion propitious for confidences, told him of having been misled into religious infidelity and of having returned to the faith, referring probably to that early period in Glasgow when he was inclining towards Catholicism, from which Sir John Pringle, the physician, was delegated by Boswell's family to reclaim him. Thereupon Johnson "called to me with warmth, 'Give me your hand; I have taken a liking to you.'" That evening they sat from nine until after one, warmed by wine and good fellowship, and never afterwards, in the more than twenty years of their relationship, were they more deeply boon companions, for even the best of friendships blossom most luxuriantly at the beginning.

"Had it been foretold to me some years ago," he was moved to declare, "that I should pass an evening with the author of "The Rambler," how should I have exulted!" Johnson was touched. "Sir, I am glad we have met. I hope we shall pass many evenings and mornings, too, together." It is on such nights as this that hearts run over into vows and pledges of eternal alliances of offense and defense. They met again at the Mitre, on July 1, with Goldsmith, to whose literary autonomy Boswell seemed perversely or stupidly blind, presenting him as "one of the brightest ornaments of the Johnsonian school." And they talked and talked, and when they parted Goldsmith accompanied Johnson to the lodgings of Mrs. Williams, with whom he was wont to drink tea every night before he went home, she staying up, however late it was. (She is sometimes referred to as Miss). "Dr. Goldsmith, being a privileged man, went with him this night, strutting away, and calling to me with an air of superiority, like that of an esoterick over an exoterick diciple of a sage of antiquity, 'I go to Miss Williams.' I confess I then envied him this mighty privilege, of which he seemed so proud; but it was not long before I obtained the same mark of distinction." That either should have regarded as a 'privilege' the sharing of tea with this poor blind woman seems either charmingly naif or eminently childish.

Four days later, Tuesday, the 5th of July, Boswell again paid Johnson a visit and the following day the younger man was host at the Mitre, Johnson, Goldsmith, Davies and two others, one a clergyman, being his guests. On Saturday, July 9th, Boswell found Johnson "surrounded with a numerous levee" and on the 14th "we had another evening by ourselves at the Mitre." He writes to his friend of Johnson's cordiality on that occasion and asks, rhetorically, in that charming manner which would disarm one's worst enemies, "Now, Temple, can I help indulging vanity?" On Tuesday, July 19th, he found "tall Sir Thomas Robinson sitting with Johnson" and they discussed the auctorial pretensions of Frederick the Great Boswell having had some trouble with the landlord of his Downing Street lodgings the night before he had been host to Johnson and having then been obliged to take his company to the Mitre, he now moved to the chambers in Farrars-buildings, at the bottom of Inner Temple Lane which had been occupied by his friend, Temple, a move which brought Boswell closer to the chief object of his veneration. Boswell entertained him there for the first time on Wednesday, July 20th, Mr. Dempster and Dr. Boswell, his uncle, being others of the company. They met on five more days during the remainder of that month alone, on one, the 30th, spending the entire day together, along the Thames, travelling to Greenwich, and ending the day at the Turk's Head Coffee House, on Gerard Street, Soho.

CHAPTER TWO

"Having Submitted to His Father's . . ."

HAVING submitted to his father's wish that he take up the law, Boswell was to go to Utrecht to perfect his knowledge of it for practice in Edinburgh, as well as to travel to the right places and see the people who counted. As the price of compliance with his father's wish that he take up the law, the young man, with patient, devious ways, wangled out of the Laird consent to a grand tour which was to give him about as much contemporary reputation in Europe as Johnson had in England. Johnson accompanied him by coach to Harwich, the embarkation point. On the evening of August 2, three days before he was to leave, Johnson took him to have tea with Mrs. Williams, a sign to Boswell that "I had now made good my title to be a privileged man." The following day they had their last social evening before Boswell's departure, at the Turk's Head, and two days later, in the morning, they took the Harwich stage coach and Boswell, aboard ship, watched Johnson on the deck, "rolling his majestick frame in his usual manner" until he disappeared in the town.

At Utrecht the young Scotch student flavored the study of law with the courtship of the brilliant frustrated Zélide (Belle de Zuylen), she who later became the Egeria of Benjamin Constant and whose letters to himself Boswell sent on to Rousseau as worthy of his perusal. It was this courtship which helped lift him out of a deep fit of despondency. In a letter he wrote to Charles de Guiffardière, he pictured the more agreeable side of Utrecht life, telling the clergyman who was to become Queen Charlotte's French reader and the Mr. Turbulent of Fanny Burney's diary of the agreeableness of Utrecht life, of its "brilliant assemblys twice a week and private partys almost every evening" and of

JAMES BOSWELL

From the drawing by George Dance in the National Portrait Gallery. From a photograph by Emery Walker

the beautiful and amiable ladies to whom he was gaining social access. That Zélide retained some hold on his affections after he had left her city for Germany is amply proven by the debate which he conducted within himself, a debate which was not decided until years afterwards.

In one of the most surprising proposals ever young man made fair lady, the ingenuous youth wrote: "Let me ask you, then, Zélide, could you submit your inclination to the opinion, perhaps the *caprice,* of a husband? Could you do this with cheerfulness, without losing any of your sweet good humor, without boasting of it? Could you live quietly in the country six months a year? Could you make yourself agreeable to plain honest neighbors? Could you talk like any other woman, and have your fancy as much at command as your harpsichord? Could you pass the other six months in a city where there is very good society, though not the high mode? Could you live thus and be content? . . . Could you give spirits to your husband when he is melancholy? I have known such wives, Zélide. What think you? Could you be such a one?" Boswell could hardly expect an all-embracing "Yes" to the dull-tinted pictures which his questions evoked in the mind's eye of the lively, sceptical, mathematical, metaphysical blue-stocking. Yet the possibility of such a marriage suggests lively and amusing vistas, for however Zélide might have served as Mrs. Boswell, her conversation would have provided him with at least several more Uxoriana than he managed to glean from the lady who did bear his name.

As Baron Boswell and as M. de Boswell he visited the courts of Germany, relishing to the last drop the life of courts, the company of princes and the homage of the people. If he failed to establish relations with Frederick the Great—one of those whom he would have loved to Boswellize—at least he danced the minuet with the Hereditary Princess of Brunswick, sister of George III. And this was clear gain, for however he may have felt about Frederick before he visited Prussia, he saw enough of the soldier-king's despotism to weaken his inclination. His cup ran over when he danced with the Princess Elizabeth, for whom he pretended so violent an attachment that he toyed with the fancy of carrying her off and thus causing a second Trojan War, with the Prince of Prussia in the role of the deserted Menelaus. Marching into Switzerland, he laid siege, with the inn at Môtiers as base, to Rousseau, who discovered, and was forced to submit to, Boswellian pertinacity. He conducted his siege for several days, ignoring Rousseau's manifest desire to be let alone. Not only did Boswell have his own way, but he obtained, beside, a dinner, a commendation for his "pleasant malice" and an introduction to Pasquale di Paoli, leader of the insurgent Corsicans against the Genoese. Rousseau told Boswell that mankind disgusted him, that Paul would have made an Anglican clergyman and that Johnson should not have accepted the pension. From Môtiers Boswell proceeded on to Ferney where, after having obtained an invitation to stay, he determined to make Voltaire a Christian and convert him to a belief in the immortality of the soul.

In Italy, his next terrain, he thought it the proper part of manhood to be a Don Juan, paying court to a number of ladies of title, including three countesses,[1] and to the mistress of his travelling companion, the young Lord Montstuart, namely Porzia Sansedoni, of whom he asked the ultimate favor as a pledge of loyalty to their mutual friend! But the Italian angel, the Signora of Siena, who continued to write to him for some years and to whom he vaguely alludes in this correspondence with Temple was none of these. She was Moma Tai, who denied him nothing, begged him not to leave her, and has the distinction, according to Geoffrey Scott, of being the only woman who ever lost her heart to Boswell. In Turin, Rome and Naples, Boswell cemented his friendship with the squint-eyed Whig and libertine whose dislike for the Scotch was more purely political than Johnson's, namely Jack Wilkes. The young traveller was paying as little attention as was convenient to letters from his father demanding his return.

Instead of obeying, he proceeded onward into Corsica, a dangerous terra incognita for any

[1] whose unimportant names the curious may find in Volume 5 of the Boswell Papers.

young gentleman finishing off a grand tour, but for the enterprising Boswell, the springboard for his leap into a European celebrity. On his return journey, he passed through Paris, where again he found Wilkes, and had an affair with Rousseau's Thérèse Levasseur, whom he brought with him to London, to meet Rousseau, who, with Hume as sponsor, had preceded them. In the quarrel that followed—in which were involved Hume and Rousseau as principals, and Boswell, Walpole, D'Alembert and Mme. de Boufflers—we have no interest for our present purpose. When Boswell returned to London his travels were largely over, but he returned an expanded and expansive man. In the avidity of his curiosity he was the master of Johnson. He could justly write: "I am, I flatter myself, compleatly a Citizen of the World. In my Travels, through Holland, Germany, Switzerland, Italy, Corsica, France, I never felt myself from home: and I sincerely love 'every kindred and tongue and people and nation.'" [2]

[2] He delighted in a cosmopolitanism which he pretended could not affect his principles. In his "Letter to the People

It was in Corsica, however, that he laid the basis for one of his enduring friendships, that with Paoli whose sponsor and advocate he was later in London, where the Corsican came in quest of refuge, bespeaking him to his sovereign and to Pitt. As history has since identified Boswell indissolubly with Johnson, so he sought, in his own time, to identify himself with Corsica and Paoli. He enjoyed a brief burst of derivatory glory as "Paoli Boswell" and as "Paoli's Englishman" and at the Shakespeare Jubilee of 1769 at Stratford-on-Avon he appeared in the costume of a Corsican chief, with a placard in his hat bearing the legend not of 'Corsica Boswell,' as the error goes, but of *"viva la Libertà,"* and then wrote an account of his appearance at the masquerade for the London Magazine. He was at this time not an unknown clown ballyhooing himself and Corsica, but an author of

of Scotland," he wrote of himself: "I can drink, I can laugh, I can converse, in perfect good humour, with Whigs, with Republicans, with Dissenters, with Independents, with Quakers, with Moravians, with Jews. They can do me no harm. My mind is made up. My principles are fixed. But I would vote with Tories and pray with a Dean and Chapter."

some distinction, for he had published, in the previous Spring, through a Glasgow firm, an "Account of Corsica, the Journal of a Tour to that Island and Memoirs of Pascal Paoli," which gave him his first taste of international literary reputation, for not only did it go through numerous editions, authorized and pirated, in England, Scotland and Ireland, but it was translated into German, Italian, Dutch and twice into French.

"The Life of Samuel Johnson" has not yet (1929) had a full translation into any alien tongue, although a Swedish translation is under way. It is amusing to note that one of the French translators deleted from Boswell all his allusions to Johnson, in view of the fact that the works of the latter were unknown on the Continent and that this matter was of no pertinence to what Boswell had to say about Corsica and Paoli. Napoleon was only the most distinguished of Boswell's readers; among Corsicans, for generations, the name of this sometimes ridiculous Scotchman was held in honor, if not in veneration.

Strengthened and enlarged by his travels, Boswell returned to London in February, 1766, three months less than three years from his first encounter of Johnson in Tom Davies's shop and found Johnson in new quarters, in Johnson's Court, No. 7 Fleet Street, in which Mrs. Williams was assigned an apartment on the ground floor, while Robert Levett, a pitiful old quack to whom Johnson also gave shelter, kept his old place in the garret, his chief function in the household apparently consisting in pouring tea for Johnson in the morning and speaking only when he was spoken to. One visitor has testified to the manner in which Johnson would toss to Levett the crust of a roll after having torn out the crumb he required for himself. Francis Barber, the Negro servant whom Sir Joshua Reynolds has immortalized on a canvas which has recently been brought to America, acted in the capacity of Johnson's body servant.

The claims Edinburgh made on Boswell were too numerous and exacting to permit him to spend very much time in London and in Johnson's company. At Edinburgh, he had not only to nurse a slowly-growing law practice, but to look after his chief mistress, that Mrs. D. . . . (also known as the Moffatt woman, from the name of the town in which he met her) whom Boswell found so admirably formed for amorous dalliance, not to mention more passing loves, such as the gardener's daughter; and his two known illegitimate children, a son whose name is believed to have been Charles and a daughter known as Sally whom Mrs. D. presented Boswell. He was at various times deeply concerned in efforts to cure himself of "the venereal disorder," not to mention slighter memoranda of vice, which he acquired even in London, in which he spent a good deal of his time elsewhere than at Johnson's feet, as is generally supposed, for it was from London that he wrote to Temple: "I am positive I shall never go astray, were it from nothing else but the absolute dread of pain. I shall be confined a week yet." He was also engaged in wife-hunting, his inclination reverting to Zélide when Miss Blair failed him, swinging to "La belle Irlandaise," and finally attaching to his cousin, Margaret Montgomerie, whom he married on that day in November, 1769, when his father chose to rewed. He had paid a short visit to Ireland, but not, as Johnson had suggested, that he might empty his head of Corsica.

On the contrary, after Genoa had sold the sovereignty of Corsica to France, Boswell renewed his efforts in the Corsican cause, attempting to enlist the sympathies of the powerful, filling the press with articles and paragraphs, many of them intended to stir up English intervention, and even going so far as to raise subscriptions and sending ordnance for use against the new enemy. When Paoli, following his defeat by the French, came to London, Boswell served him as spokesman and it was to Boswell's influence that Walpole attributed the grant to the Corsican of an annual pension of 1000 pounds. It was the general's house rather than Johnson's, that Boswell used as his headquarters during his London visits. As late as 1776 Boswell was indicating to Temple that he planned to work up this "memorabilia Paoli," he had been collecting, showing that Johnson was not always the single, fixed object of his idolatry. Indeed, Professor Tinker asserts that Boswell felt a deeper reverence for Paoli than for Johnson. The more we learn about Boswell as an independent entity the more we become aware of the obligations, diversions and ambitions which militated against his exclusive service to Johnson—the rearing of a family, the nurturing of a law practice, the maintenance of a large correspondence, and his triumphs and errors in political journalism, related forms of prose, and poetry.

Ambition, duty, necessity, caprice combined to keep Boswell and Johnson apart, perhaps not entirely to the older man's distaste. When Boswell was out of Johnson's sight he may not have been out of Johnson's mind, but he was not sufficiently included in the favor of his correspondence. During a large part of Boswell's European tour—1764 and 1765—Johnson "did not favour me with a single letter" and during 1770 also there was not a single exchange. There were other separations, equally long, unbridged, or only tenuously bridged, from Johnson's side of the Tweed, with correspondence.

In 1773 or ten years after their first meeting, Boswell dined with Johnson, in Johnson's room, for the first time, finding the table far less uncouth than he had supposed it would be. That year, however, is memorable for the fact that in the Fall they undertook their fruitful tour of the Hebrides, during which Johnson visited the Boswells at their Edinburgh home and, subsequently, the Laird himself, Boswell's father, at Auchinleck, winning the affection neither of his disciple's wife nor father.

The Laird was hurt that Jamie should have tied himself to the tail of: "A dominie, an auld dominie, that keepit a schule and ca'd it an academy," and Mrs. Boswell, disturbed by such odd habits of Johnson's as burning lighted candles upside down when in the parlor to make them burn the better, was moved to remark: "I have seen many a bear led by a man: but I never before saw a man led by a bear." It was not until some time afterwards that Mrs. Boswell indicated forgiveness, if not forgetfulness, by sending the bear, or Ursa Major, some marmalade of oranges, although honey would better have carried on the analogy. But perhaps Goldsmith's answer to the question: "Who is this Scotch cur at Johnson's heels?" is a more graphic description of the relationship: "He is not a cur, but is only a bur. Tom Davies flung him at Johnson in sport, and he has the faculty of sticking."

For twenty-one years Boswell stuck to Johnson, until he died, in 1784. They met for the last time on June 30, 1784 at dinner at Sir Joshua Reynolds. Boswell accompanied him back in the coach from Leicester Square to Bolt Court. "We bade adieu to each other affectionately in the carriage. When he had got down upon the foot pavement he called out 'Fare you well,' and without looking back, sprung away with a kind of pathetic briskness, if I may use that expression, which seemed to indicate a struggle to conceal uneasiness, and impressed one with a foreboding of our long, long separation."

And even the years after his death, even up to Boswell's own, were Johnson's, even if other claims were acknowledged and met. The Great Cham of Literature died on the evening of December 13, 1784, in his 76th year, and was laid to rest in Westminster Abbey. Eleven years elapsed before Boswell was to join his friend and a good deal of that time was devoted to his great book. It would have been a sufficiently creative achievement to have written the "Life," but Boswell completed, in addition, a gigantic task of news gathering and organization, his triumph being the more notable when we consider that "The Life of Samuel Johnson" was not his only occupation, or avocation, during the years when the raw data was being gathered, organized and creatively transformed into the finished book. Of his competitors in Johnsoniana he seemed to fear but two, Mrs. Thrale-Piozzi, author of the still lively "Anecdotes," and the unclubbable Sir John Hawkins, whose official "Life," perversely commended by men who should know better, only throws into sharper relief the magnitude of Boswell's achievement.

In 1784 Boswell moved to London, he having two years before become head of Auchinleck by the Laird's death. Five years later he became a widower and he allowed old habits to resume

THE VAUNTING JAMES BOSWELL

From a contemporary caricature of the biographer on his home grounds, Scotland, the "land of stones"

their sway over him, falling prey to his love of liquor and his strong inclination to hypochondria. Besides, he permitted debts to bear him down so heavily that he even entertained a proposal to sell his interest in the "Life" for 1000 pounds. As one of the henchmen of the brutal politician, Lord Lonsdale, he obtained the Recordership of Carlisle but was disappointed in his hope of being named to a seat in Parliament. The political chapter in Boswell's life is particularly depressing, as his letters to Temple show. There was a time when his heart was more deeply set on practicing before the English bar and sitting in Parliament than in completing "The Life of Samuel Johnson." Boswell died in his house at No. 47 Great Portland Street, on May 19, 1795, fifty-five years of age, three days after the 32d anniversary of his first meeting with Johnson.

The first edition of his great "Life" was published May 16, 1791, the twenty-eighth anniversary of the encounter in Davies's shop. Tormented by the difficulties of his task though he had been, and dubious, later on, of the prospect of success, he felt, once the " Life " was in press, that it would be, as he wrote to Temple, " without exception, the most entertaining book you ever read," and when it was published the world agreed, for he gave the world, as he had promised Temple, not only " a *history* of Johnson's *visible* progress through the world, and of his publications, but a *view* of his mind, in his letters and conversations," the whole making "*more* of a *Life* than any work that ever yet appeared." And at the time of his last illness he was engaged in preparing the third edition, the completion of which devolved upon his friend, Edmond Malone, the great Shakespearian scholar, the man who stood over Boswell's shoulder from the very beginning of the enterprise and transfused his faith and courage into the veins of the flabby, faltering Boswell. The third edition of 1799 remained the basic edition until 1887 when Dr. George Birkbeck Hill displaced it and the intervening editions of Malone and of John Wilson Croker by his edition, a monumental work of annotated erudition, in the preface of which the editor, applying a remark of Johnson's in the preface to the Shakespeare edition, suggests to the newcomer to Boswell to read his Boswell straight, without hindrance of footnotes.

When Johnson died he was Boswell's and long before Boswell died he had been Johnson's. Never before, nor since, except in legend, have the destinies of two men been so inextricably interwoven. Two stags with antlers locked in death do not belong one to the other more completely than Boswell and Johnson. The language needs a composite word made from their names to indicate the nature of the interdependence which their lives symbolizes. History has no comparable example of interdependence. We cannot imagine one existing without the other. Think of one, the other rises to the mind as an inevitable corollary. Write or speak the name of either, the name of the other follows effortlessly. Boswell's wish to attach his own superficially silly name and pretensions to those of authentic greatness was realized even beyond the dreams of avarice-in-ambition, but with an ironic accent that makes it hard to say whose was the greater gain. Perhaps the chief irony in this relation and in its consequences is that the man who, to his own generation, seemed so self-reliant, so self-sufficient, so sure of posterity's suffrage; that the man whose death "kept the public mind in agitation beyond all former example," should be indebted for his flourishing life-after-death to one who had been put down as a fool, a toad-eater, a tale-bearer, a conceited ass, unsnubbable, superstitious, insolent; in short, contemptible—in life, but, in death, an immortal. An immortal ass, maybe, but immortal, if only through the words deriving from his name which have found places in the Dictionary —another joke which the great Lexicographer would have keenly relished. What Gray wrote to Walpole about Bozzy's Corsican book—that "any fool may write a most valuable book by chance"—Macaulay applied to everything Boswell wrote, giving chance all the innings and Boswell none. Perhaps Boswell gave a commentator like Macaulay some reason for putting him down as a fool but no one who ponders Boswell's share in the conversations he has made immortal, who notes the patience and industry with which he fed the greater man occasions for great speech, and remarks the acuteness with which he differed with Johnson and on how many occasions he took the side of liberty and toleration when Johnson was thumping for constituted authority—no one then can deny him a goodly share of intelligence. He had a temperamental, if not intellectual, unconventionality. Johnson declared him to be the best traveling companion in the world and said that he regarded him as a man who "never left a house without leaving a wish for his return," and commended his acuteness of mind, gaiety of conversation and civility of manner. "He (Boswell) has better faculties than I had imagined," Johnson wrote to Mrs. Thrale from Auchinleck; "more justness of discernment, and more fecundity of images."

And even if we were to dismiss Johnson's commending phrases as to the purchase of sheer devotion rather than of worth, we of this generation, better than his own, or Macaulay's, shall be enabled to declare and to define Boswell's chief merits. For the publication, in no less than sixteen volumes, of the Private Papers of James Boswell, purchased from his great-great-grandson, Lord Talbot de Malahide, and made accessible to Johnsonians by the purchaser, Col. Ralph E. Isham, will help us to revise our conception of Boswell as a Johnsonian make-weight. It is likely that he who made Johnson the most intimately-known figure of history will be found to have done himself a like service. Boswell is emerging as a personality in his own right. These diaries and letters which have come out of Boswell's ebony cabinet, added to the letters he wrote to Temple and others, will serve to put Boswell by the side of Pepys, for no more than the little diarist of the Admiralty did Boswell serve the reticences. These papers are justifying the faith of those who had felt that Boswell also was a vivid and various personality. At the very least we shall be supplied with some fascinating footnotes to the large body of Boswelliana already in our possession. We shall be informed, in somewhat fuller detail, of Boswell's rich, independent non-Johnsonion life. Frederick Albert Pottle's bibliography of Boswell, "The

Literary Career of James Boswell, Esq.," opens our eyes to the magnitude of Boswell's literary industry, the variety of his literary enterprises and the justification for his literary reputation; it stresses the non-Johnsonian aspect of Boswell's life from a literary point of view as new knowledge of his life stresses that aspect from a personal point of view. When the publication of The Boswell Papers shall have been completed we shall have not only new material on such of Johnson's contemporaries as Reynolds, Goldsmith and Burke, but also—what the late Geoffrey Scott, who had been editing those volumes up to the time of his sudden death regarded as most important—the record of Boswell's post-Johnson life. Not since Boswell's letters to Temple came to light seventy years ago as waste-paper in a Boulogne shop has a finer collection of source material fallen into a collector's hands. We are to have, in the rough, the autobiography of James Boswell—in all its implications—an autobiography no matter how thickly overlaid with the trivial. But this will help us to the new perception of Johnson as a golden incident, but an incident, in Boswell's life, as Boswell was an incident in Johnson's. The survival of Johnson's greatness under the pressure of Boswell's familiarity is prima facie evidence of that greatness; by the same token Boswell is an interesting person, for he cannot sate our interest in himself; the more he gives us the more he feeds the flame of curiosity. Prof. Walter Raleigh has put Boswell into a gifted phrase, "He was an amateur of human life" and explains his success by another, "He had the art of interesting others without incurring their respect." Conscious that he was held in contempt, Boswell, writing of himself in the third person in his "Journal of a Tour to the Hebrides," declared with justice, "he had thought more than anybody supposed, and had a pretty good stock of general learning and knowledge." The new portrait of Boswell may lose the simplicity of its old outlines, because it will be subjected inevitably to contradictions, just as the mass of material we have on Johnson obliges us to reconcile contradictions which might not otherwise have been made apparent.

CHAPTER THREE

"When Did Boswell Decide . . ."

WHEN did Boswell decide to Boswellize Johnson and thus Johnsonize the English-speaking world? That he made notes on Johnson's talk from the very first is apparent to any reader of the "Life." What is not apparent is that he was readier to take notes and whip them into shape for his Journal than he was to organize his material into such lasting form as he gave to the life and letters, work and conversation of Samuel Johnson, LL. D. Large as is the bulk of Boswell's writings, his path was strewn with the scattered leaves of planned, projected but unfinished, biographies of his contemporaries. But the ambition to stand in the shadows cast by his distinguished elders without being himself blotted out and to contract their wisdom in his note books had its origin in Scotland, while he was engaged in study at Edinburgh and Glasgow universities and combating the tedium of life by paying court to such celebrities as Kames, Blair, Hume, Robertson and Sir David Dalrymple. At the age of eighteen he had already met the distinguished historian and "infidel" Hume. But it was upon Sir David, a friend of the family, a jurist and an historian for whom Johnson later said some kind words, that Boswell tried his biographical eye-teeth. Before Boswell even saw Johnson he had kept a brief account of Sir David's sayings on the Northern circuit. He long played with the notion of writing Kames's life. An equal distinction might have fallen upon Sir Alexander Dick, a neighbor of Auchinleck and a friend of the family, whom Boswell, as potential biographer, several times interviewed, but for Boswell's incapacity to achieve the full measure of his plans. Boswell was so promiscuous in his biographical affections and so ingenuously inclined to make plans and resolutions which his sometimes flabby will could not hope to execute, that his loyalty to Johnson, strong as it was, might not have been strong enough to produce the "Life." It is posterity, impregnated with the Boswell-Johnson "aether," that has simplified the crowded lives of subject and biographer.

When he stood before Johnson in the back room of Davies's shop, Boswell was by no means unprepared for the task of recording and treasuring the sayings that might fall from the Doctor's lips, and he must have been encouraged in the hope of indulging his desire after the not uncordial reception which he received upon his first call at Johnson's chambers. And when we consider how strong was the satellitic impulse in Boswell and what fine qualities he possessed as a foil and drawer-out, it is not inconceivable that had Johnson rebuffed the almost unrebuffable Boswell, he would have made his reputation—if not preserved Johnson's—by attending in a like capacity upon some other celebrity. Indeed, so little did Boswell at that time regard Johnson as the exclusive object of his biographical concern that within two months after their fateful first meeting of May 16, "that biographical, anecdotical memorandummer" had begun collecting anecdotes about Wilkes.

And when he returned from his European tour, he had with him the rough material for his book on Corsica and Paoli, copious notes of his interviews with Rousseau and Voltaire, data on his most distinguished travelling companion, George Keith, the Earl Marischal of Scotland, a romantic figure for biography; and, in all likelihood, additional data on Wilkes, whom he had met in Italy. Had Johnson failed him, or had his will and industry been equal to his opportunities, he might have Boswellized, at greater detail, the colorful Oglethorpe, Hume, but, better than these, Jack Wilkes. I regard the book that Boswell might have done about Wilkes as one of the greatest unwritten biographies in the English language. He was Wilkes the witty, Wilkes the dangerous, Wilkes the libertine—rebellious pamphleteer, the idol of the populace who drove Bute from the right hand of King George and who, as Lord Mayor of London, defended the colonists and refused to lend horses to the king's heralds who were to proclaim the colonists traitors.

He was, in many respects, more congenial if less to be reverenced and hearkened to, than Johnson, and Wilkes, like Barkus, would have been willin'. It is by no mere coincidence, however, that Boswell's best books are about virtuous men, Paoli and Johnson, although he was no hypocrite in the pleasure he felt in the company of libertines.

It was at the grave of Melanchton, at the Wittemberg church where the Reformation was first preached, that Boswell pledged himself to the great service. On Sunday, September 30, 1764, lying flat on his stomach, the paper pressing against the epitaph and with a group of wondering villagers looking on, he wrote his letter of fealty to Johnson. Therein, he said in part: "At this tomb, then, my ever dear and respected friend, I vow to thee an eternal attachment. It shall be my study to do what I can to render your life happy: and, if you die before me, I shall endeavor to do honour to your memory." This was the histrionic Boswell, putting himself in a romantic pose, but, for once, the pledge was exceeded by the fidelity of the deed. When they were at Auchinleck, during the Hebridean journey, Boswell expressed the intention "to erect a monument to him here," but with his constitutional dread of the theme of death, Johnson "turned off the subject, saying, 'Sir, I hope to see your grand children.'" From Edinburgh on Feb. 24, 1777, Boswell wrote: "Be assured, my dear Sir, that my affection and reverence for you are exalted and steady. I do not believe that a more perfect attachment ever existed in the history of mankind." With that we agree. And on the 24th of August, 1780, he wrote to Johnson: "I would willingly have ten years added to my life, to have ten taken away from yours; I mean, that I would be ten years older to have you ten years younger."

Boswell's "Life" has so thoroughly soaked into the minds of English-speaking peoples that it is almost impossible to imagine our literature without it. It has penetrated English literature not only through itself, but also through the numerous by-products which have been derived therefrom, the debt not having to be acknowl-

THE SOMETIMES INSEPARABLE TWO

Johnson and Boswell taking a walk, as pictured by the famous caricaturist, Thomas Rowlandson

edged since the source is not only the common possession of the English-speaking race, but the unconsciously common possession. The "Life" is rich in anecdotes and repartees which have become our common heritage in such a manner that the person reading it for the first time must feel like the young woman who upon hearing "Romeo and Juliet" for the first time declared it a play full of quotations. Because of Boswell, Johnson survives as the best known, most intimately known, human figure in history. Whatever the newly published Boswell Papers may add to our knowledge of Boswell they can take away nothing from our knowledge of Johnson —they will indeed add to it, directly and indirectly. Without Boswell, we should be wondering by what accident, by what freak of chance a man by the name of Samuel Johnson happens to be lying in Westminster Abbey. Quite a number of students of English literature would know, but not the race, not as it knows today and knew yesterday and will know tomorrow. Examination of what Johnson himself wrote—even of his best—is a sufficiently novel experience, yet, but for Boswell, we never would have felt the compulsion to undertake such an examination. And some of us who have, have marvelled at the manner in which a dead writer and a living personality can subsist within one another.

Never before and never since has purely contemporary reputation been projected into the future on the basis of such meagre literary distinction—assayed apart from his personality—as was Johnson's. Whatever Johnson's purely literary distinction, it is a meagre one against the reputation of Johnson the personality. What Johnson wrote was for his age; what Boswell wrote about Johnson has long survived the term allotted to a contemporary classic. Johnson was the greatest personality of his time and because he was little more than that he would have been doomed to double extinction with his death—under normal conditions.[1] He

[1] It was after I had reached this independent conclusion on the mortality of Johnson's writings that I came across Leslie Stephen's essay in which he presents the same view, and even more extremely. "And thus but for the inimitable Boswell, it must be admitted that Johnson would probably have sunk very deeply into oblivion. A few good sayings

need not have feared death with such mortal terror had he anticipated the Boswellian contribution and its effect in insuring him against spiritual dissolution. During the Hebridean journey, Johnson regularly looked over Boswell's journal, and on one occasion remarked: "It grows better and better . . . It might be printed, were the subject fit for printing." But it pleased him to know that the labors of his conversation were being hoarded. "The more I read of this," he said to Boswell, after looking over further instalments, "I think the more highly of you." Fortunately, Boswell realized what constituted fitness for printing. Read Bos-

---

would have been preserved by Mrs. Thrale and others, or have been handed down by tradition, and doubtless assigned in process of time to Sidney Smith and other conversational celebrities. A few couplets from the "Vanity of Human Wishes" would not yet have been submerged, and curious readers would have recognized the power of "Rasselas," and been delighted with some shrewd touches in the "Lives of the Poets." But with all desire to magnify critical insight, it must be admitted that that man would have shown singular penetration, and been regarded as an eccentric commentator, who had divined the humour and fervour of mind which lay hid in the remains of the huge lexicographer."

well's report of this journey, which took but a few months, and consider what "The Life of Samuel Johnson, LL. D." would have been had the companionship of this precious pair been subjected to fewer and briefer separations. We are rich in what Boswell gave us and poor only by comparison with the treasure we might have had. Boswell complained to his friend Temple that Johnson did not wish him to publish a book on the Hebrides, since his had just been issued. A comparison of Johnson's report of that journey with Boswell's justifies Johnson's fears, for whoever wishes to make out a case for Boswellian superiority in observation cannot do better than look at these two reports of one journey. Boswell was obedient, however. His "Journal of a Tour to the Hebrides" did not appear until nine months after the death of the author of "A Journey to the Western Islands of Scotland."

In his complaint to Temple, Boswell wrote: "Between ourselves, he is not apt to encourage one to *share* reputation with himself." Surely, the literary angels must laugh at a terrestrial joke on so cosmic a scale. Who, if not

Johnson, has been obliged to share reputation? Indeed Boswell salvaged him from death and gave him to posterity. If we accept Macaulay's definition of Boswell as a small man, then the big thing that is The Life of Johnson is a miracle, and it is the custom of this age to reject miracles. All knowledge of, all interest in, the literary and social aspects of the Johnsonian period derives from, and returns to, Boswell, the great source. Without him, the epoch would have lacked the name and the personality it has. It took the American Revolution to prevent our forgetting that George III reigned in Johnson's time. Boswell perfectly fulfilled his destiny and, in fulfilling it, fulfilled another man's, projected Johnson into the ages. "Homer is not more decidedly the first of heroic poets," wrote Macaulay, "Shakespeare is not more decidely the first of dramatists, Demosthenes is not more decidedly the first of orators, than Boswell is the first of biographers. He has no second. He has distanced all his competitors so decidedly that it is not worth while to place them. Eclipse is first and the rest nowhere." Discount a little from this, on the assumption of Macaulayian exaggeration, and the "Life" yet remains a great work.

The year 1763 may justly be regarded as central in the lives of Johnson and Boswell. And it may consequently be regarded as the central year in the Johnsonian epoch, which one writer on the period, Thomas Seccombe, dates as having begun in 1748, which year saw the publication of Hume's "Inquiry Concerning the Human Understanding," Samuel Richardson's "Clarissa Harlowe," Tobias Smollett's "Roderick Random" and John and Charles Wesley's "Hymns for the Lord's Supper." The Johnsonian age was distinguished chiefly by—aside from Johnson—the rise of Methodism, the establishment of the modern novel, as exemplified by the works of Richardson and Fielding; the beginning of the Romantic movement in literature, and acceleration in the development of modern industry, which was being pushed along the road toward its present goal by the inventions of Hargreaves's spinning-jenny, Arkwright's water-frame, Crompton's "mule" and Watt's steam-engine. Meadows and villages were being converted by the "dark, Satanic mills" of pubescent Industrialism into towns like Manchester, Leeds, Birmingham and Sheffield. The isolated communities which formed the England of the pre-Johnson era were being knit together by the opening of hundreds of miles of canals and of roads. "The convenience of turnpike-roads" Hawkins observed, "has destroyed the distinction between town and country manners." Although Industrialism did not reach its maturity in Johnson's life-time, it had proceeded far enough to enable him to observe that, among other things, "it also hurts the bodies of the people."

Methodism was to serve as a civilizing and purifying influence on language, morals and manners of middle and lower classes, foreshadowing, if not preparing the ground for, Victorianism. The royal house was declining in prestige, the grubby domesticity of the third George and his Queen eliciting no great bursts of affection. Indeed, even after Culloden when the claims of the Pretender, Prince Charles Edward, were smothered in blood and dust, the royal house of Hanover was tolerated in silence rather than proclaimed by huzzahs. One of the chief marks of disrespect which the third George was obliged to suffer was "The Lousiad," the "epic" of John Wolcott ("Peter Pindar") which was occasioned by a royal order that the servants have their heads shaved, following an unhappy experience with the royal soup. Wilkes was perhaps a more inconvenient fly in the royal ointment, being the occasion for riots in his favorite bailiwicks, Middlesex, which thrice re-elected him to Parliament, and London, which made him Lord Mayor.

The Johnsonian age was the testing time for innovations. A growing reading public was making the patron less necessary, if not entirely dispensable, and increasing importance was being attached to opinion printed as against the spoken opinion at coffee houses in the "Town." Circulating libraries were coming into use. Wrote the bookseller Lackington: "A number of book clubs are also formed in every part of England where each member subscribes a certain sum quarterly to purchase books." Improving literature, fiction with a moral purpose, was becoming popular. Women were taking up reading in a serious way, not to mention writing. Horace Walpole's "The Castle of Otranto" introduced the Gothic note into romance, and William Beckford was to match a Fonthill Abbey for a Strawberry Hill and a "Vathek" for an "Otranto." Cheap reprints of classical works were being bought and booksellers not only were becoming respectable, a few of them were acquiring coaches, the aforementioned Lackington owing a considerable part of his success to Wesley's policy of popularizing knowledge in the form of outlines. The plethora of anti-Methodist tracts and books did no harm to the bookselling trade. The science of advertising was developing, if it may be called a science. The positions of magazine and newspaper were becoming consolidated. Careers were becoming more accessible to talents, as witness not only Garrick, Reynolds and Johnson, but Dodsley, ex-footman, poet and bookseller. Enterprising booksellers, creating, or being created by, the larger reading public were making it possible for the writer to know a somewhat better lot than " toil, envy, want, the patron and the jail," although Johnson suffered some of these in his early years. One of these entrepreneurs of literature, William Strahan, who had purchased a share of the patent for King's Printer, sat in Parliament from 1774 to 1783, and it was upon another of the same trade, Andrew Millar, and not upon some wealthy nobleman, that Johnson bestowed the epithet, " the Maecenas of the age." And there was that minor Maecenas, that bustling " Jack Whirler " of Johnson's essay who sold not only books but such nostrums as Dr. James's Fever Powders, the favorite patent medicine of the age. Newbery we remember chiefly because he was the first bookseller who made a business of issuing books intended for children, Goldsmith, it is suspected, having written several of the productions Newbery marketed.

Who was who and what was what in the central year of 1763? The French and Indian War came to an end, and the foundations were laid for England's over-seas empire, for in that year the Treaty of Paris consolidated England's gains in Asia and America and she began taking a longer breath than had been permitted her in some time. Christopher Smart was shut up a second time in Bedlam, causing Johnson to wonder at the fine shades between sanity and insanity, and in Bedlam conceived the lyrical "Song to David," although legend had it that he indented the glowing verses with a key on the panels of his cell and shaded them with charcoal. And about the same time, William Cowper was placed in Dr. Cotton's asylum at St. Albans, being released in 1765 after eighteen months. Many years later he was to express, in a letter to William Unwin, his contempt for Johnson for his treatment of Milton in his "Lives of the Poets." "Oh," he wrote, "I could thresh his old jacket till I made his pension jingle in his pocket." Cowper and Smart were locked up not for the offense of being among the most lyrical poets in a prosy age, but for carrying to excess their faith at a time when religious enthusiasm was regarded as unfashionably methodistic, if not Popish.

Hume, sceptic historian, got a post in the British Embassy in Paris and became the pet of the salons, and Jack Wilkes, by his smashing attacks in the North Briton, forced Lord Bute, prime minister, out of office and made himself the specific object of a general warrant issued for his arrest. In 1763, Lady Mary Wortley Montagu, dead but a year, had her personality projected through the posthumous publications of her letters. It was a year of literary consciousness of the past. James Macpherson ("Ossian") had published "Fingal" the previous year and, in this, came "Temora" and the feud between the Ossianites and Johnson raged hot, Johnson acquiring a cudgel six feet long in preparation for any reprisal which his dismissal of "Ossian" as a forgery might bring upon his head. He was to write to Macpherson in January of 1775: "I will not desist from detecting what I think a cheat from any fear of the menaces of a Ruffian." Percy, he of the "Reliques," who later acquired an Irish bishopric and called Boswell names for daring to use the names of living men in his Johnsonian anecdotes, published in that year "Five Pieces of Runic Poetry," and Chatterton, aged eleven, was the following year to publish some satiric poems in Bristol journals and to die, five years later, after having left the Rowley fragments which are none the less poetry for being detected forgeries. Smollett, prize hack of the age, whose journalism had been found wanting when it had been called upon to save his employer, Lord Bute, was writing the volumes of a History of England. The following year, Gibbon, at Rome, was to conceive the plan of writing the History of the Decline and Fall of the Roman Empire, the first volume of which was to appear in the first year of American independence, in which issue Johnson and Gibbon were almost alone among English men of intellectual eminence in their loyalty to King, while the rest led on by Burke, and closing with Boswell, were in support of the Colonies.

In 1763, Goethe, Alfieri and Laplace were fourteen years old, the young Sheridan who was to become one of the latter shining lights of The Club, was but twelve, he having had the honor to be born in the year in which the French Encyclopaedia was inaugurated. The British Museum had been established but ten years. This was also the age of Thomas Bewick, Crabbe the poet was nine, Godwin, Raeburn and Mozart were seven, Blake and Romilly were six and a lexicographer greater than Johnson,—namely, Noah Webster—was then but five. Nelson was of the same age and two other voices of the new age, Burns and Schiller, were but four. Handel had been interred in Westminster Abbey but four years, six years after the world premiere of The Messiah in the chapel of good-hearted Captain Coram's Foundling Hospital. Bolingroke, one of the ornaments of the preceding literary reign, had been dead twelve years, Fielding nine, Jonathan Edwards five and Richardson but two. Rousseau had published his "Nouvelle Héloïse" three years before and the "Contrat Social" the year before. The new style calendar had been in operation in Britain for eleven years. Wedgewood ware came in the year in

THE RUGGED JOHNSON

From an etching, after a drawing by Ozias Humphry

which Lady Mary Wortley Montagu died, Romney came to London, André Chenier was born and the Cock Lane ghost exposed. It was the year also in which Johnson obtained his pension. The last days of George II were the great days of the elder Pitt, deposed for Bute. Six years before Boswell met Johnson, Clive defeated the enemy at Plassey and, four years before, Wolfe climbed the Heights of Abraham and, dying, took Quebec for his king.

It was towards Johnson's last years that some of this glory was to depart. "Perhaps no nation not absolutely conquered has declined so much in so short a time," he wrote to his old friend, Dr. Taylor, in August, 1782. Concessions had to be granted to Ireland, the American colonies were surrendered, rumors of landings by the French set national nerves on edge, and there was trouble besides with Holland and Spain. Incidentally, Burgoyne's surrender at Saratoga made it impossible for that literary general to be admitted as a member of The Club, even years after Johnson's death, although Boswell's influence was brought to bear on his side.

How much the character of the Johnsonian age explains the elevation of Johnson to literary dictatorship and how much this elevation is to be attributed to sheer, un-Spenglerian chance I cannot venture to say, but it was an age of prose, an age in which even poetry was prose, and in which the voices of the rebel poets were still in childish treble. It was a Victorian age, an age so torpid in its faith that it required Wesley's lash, an age which spent itself for expanding empire and industry, an age which, in poetry and fiction looked to the past because it lacked vital resources in its own time. It was the age of iron, it was the age of Johnson, an age which, but for Boswell, would have left indifferent wracks behind. Boswell the romantic made it the golden age of biography.

CHAPTER FOUR

"The Meeting of Boswell and Johnson . . ."

THE meeting of Boswell and Johnson constituted the most important cross-roads encounter in literature, but in what manner did one influence the other? To begin with, in what manner did Boswell influence Johnson? From a literary point of view, not at all. When Boswell met Johnson the latter was fifty-four years of age. The poems in which, as it was then believed, he had out-Poped Pope, and the papers constituting the Idler and the Rambler were behind him. So also was his own venture into fiction, "Rasselas," written to pay for his mother's funeral and to discharge her last debts. His Dictionary of the English Language had been published in 1755 and eight years later he complacently told some admirers, Boswell included, that the Academia della Crusca of Florence "could scarcely believe that it was done by one man." Only three more works of any consequence were yet to come from his pen, "Journey to the Western Islands of Scotland" his edition of Shakespeare, with its vigorous Preface, and the "Lives of the Poets," a characterstic work of criticism and biography undertaken at the request of a delegation of booksellers. The pension of 300 pounds a year which he was receiving from the Crown and much of which he employed in alleviating the sufferings of others, freed him from the necessity of writing for a living. He loved to talk and in inciting Johnson to talk Boswell was indulging him in the activity he loved best. Not only his best recorded talk but the bulk of his correspondence dates from that year of pensioned release. And had Johnson talked less and written more, for lack of a Boswell, even his own time would have suffered loss. Johnson, even without Boswell, would have been a better known personality than Swift, or Addison, or Pope. His talk was faithfully recorded by others of a recording turn of mind. But these others put down what he would have said anyway whereas Boswell helped " create " Johnson's talk by asking questions upon which, but for him, Johnson might not have exercised his intelligence, wit and force.

Even in his early days he did not write without a groan. "You may well wonder!" he said to a lady who wondered that he preferred not to write. And on the Scottish journey he expressed surprise that " so many people have written who might have let it alone " whereas excellence in conversation earned the instant reverberation of praise. " No man but a blockhead," said he, on another occasion, " ever wrote, except for money." When, at Oxford, in 1776, someone suggested that he write a book expressly in support of Church and State, he burst out: " Why should *I* be allways writing? " From Edmund Hector, one of Johnson's Birmingham friends, Boswell obtained the following anecdote, which illustrates his distaste for writing. In Birmingham, some years before he came to London, Johnson had been commissioned to translate from the French a "Voyage to Abyssinia," by a Portuguese Jesuit, Jerome Lobo, and, in time, he furnished the printer with the first part of his translation; "but his constitutional indolence soon prevailed and the work was at a stand." Mr. Hector, "who knew that a motive of humanity would be the most prevailing argument with his friend, went to Johnson, and represented to him that the printer could have no other employment till this undertaking was finished and that the poor man and his family were suffering." Then Johnson, for the sake of the printer's family, if not of himself, finished the job. This is the Johnson who picked up a starving girl from the London gutter and gave her refuge in his home for many weeks, who sheltered Levett and blind Mrs. Williams and Miss Carmichael and Mrs. Desmoulins and sent his Negro servant to be educated and helped rescue Goldsmith from the bailiffic wrath of an unpaid landlady and put pennies into the hands of sleeping waifs so that when they awoke they would find the price of a breakfast, and spent himself in dozens of similar services even when in deep need himself. But in London, at the height of his power, he could indulge his love of talk without forgoing the indulgence of his humane impulses.

Robust of frame though he seemed, he was physically ill for the greater part of his life, and mentally ill, too. He was tormented by the fear of insanity and death, haunted by an exacting conscience. He would prolong talk, rather than cut it short, once talk was launched, for according to Boswell's experience, he rarely spoke until he was addressed and he would sometimes lose himself in a book if the company were not pleasing to him. During such periods as he was not an abstainer, he would drink wine as a substitute for companionship, " to get rid of myself, to send myself away." His love of tavern life and his organization of clubs had a similar psychological intention. He was at some tavern until late, at Mrs. William's before she took up her quarters with him, at the Thrales' later; in the morning he was the center of a levee. Whatever inconvenience he suffered in providing shelter to his nondescript crew, they at least provided him with company, voluntary or involuntary, grateful or ungrateful. Mrs. Thrale tells of his "vehement lamentations and piercing reproofs" to her not to leave the room, and of how he would sometimes compel her to sit up and make tea for him until four in the morning. Sir Joshua has testified: "Solitude to him was terrible; nor would he ever trust himself alone, but when employed in writing or reading. He has often begged me to go home with him to prevent his being alone in the coach. Any company was better than none; by which Johnson connected himself with many mean persons whose presence he could command." The crabbed Hawkins likewise remarks upon this Johnsonian characteristic, regarding it as the hardly pardonable weakness of a great man who did not put a sufficient price on his society. The puritanical knight tells us: "The visits of idle, and some of them very worthless persons, were never unwelcome to him; and though they interrupted him in his studies and meditations, yet, as they gave him opportunities of discourse, and furnished him with intelligence, he strove rather to protract than shorten or discountenance them."

From another source we learn that Johnson had the habit of accompanying down the first flight of stairs those who, he hoped, would prolong their stay, and Hawkins tells us with what unwilling steps he would go to his lodgings from club meetings too early adjourned.

Therefore, once Johnson had put Boswell in his place, and kept him there, there was no danger that he would resent his unique courtship. And even had he not feared solitude, Johnson did the wiser thing—with a Boswell at his right hand—in enacting the oracle and puting down the pen. Mrs. Thale, of whose household Johnson became a member during Boswell's foreign tour, testifies: "His life . . . consisted in little else than talking when he was not absolutely employed in some serious piece of work, and whatever work he did seemed so much below his powers of performance that he appeared the idlest of human beings." Johnson, who had written "The Vanity of Human Wishes," was not unaware of the vanity of authorship, and it has been contended that his style underwent no change, no development, that his auctorial manner was fixed in the very first bit of writing he did for publication, the preface to the aforementioned translation from Lobo, issued anonymously as respecting the translator. It has indeed the authentic Johnsonian rumble.

Since Johnson has survived as talker and not as writer, Boswell's service to Johnson more than overbalances Johnson's to Boswell. To be sure, that style became refined and strengthened but the measured tread of his Latinity is in it. Boswell preserved and catapulted Johnson into the future in his characteristic expression—and magnificently. Boswell's influence was exerted to the delight and the instruction of posterity, rather than to Johnson's. Would it please that devout shade, that superstitious shade to know that partly because of Boswell he was surviving today as one of the great comic characters of literature, somewhere between Gargantua and Sir John Falstaff? That is what has happened. That it happened in consequence of Johnson's attempt to escape the sick, morbid, frightened part of himself, that part of him which could pray with a clergyman that God keep him sane, that part which wrote the often moving " Prayers and Meditations " is beside the point. Garrick said that Johnson " gives you a forcible hug and shakes laughter out of you whether you will or no," and Garrick, hardly less great a mimic than Foote, the comedian of the age, should be able to judge in such matters. Mrs. Thrale recorded that " no man told a story with so good a grace, or knew so well what would make an effect upon his auditors," and that none " loved laughing better, and his vein of humour was rich and apparently inexhaustible." She quoted another commentator to the effect that Johnson "was incomparable at buffoonery." Hannah More has told of the peals of laughter which the jocosity of " the old genius " evoked, and Fanny Burney said: " Dr. Johnson has more fun, and comical humour, and love of nonsense about him, than almost anybody I ever saw." I use the word comic in the large humane sense. Speaking academically, Johnson does not belong in the catalogue of English comic characters. We laugh at, as well as with, Falstaff; we admire Johnson and rejoice with him in his triumphs, in the major triumph of his life and in the minor triumphs of the tavern arena.

Perhaps Boswell, in his goggle-eyed attendance upon this Polyphemus of his does more closely suggest the obviously comical fellow, the one who elicits the good-natured laughter of tolerant contempt. He did not regard the Doctor except with respect and reverence. He was mostly the great Lexicographer, the gloomy philosopher, the stern moralist. Boswell reverenced Johnson; he did not slap him on the back, however much he may have rejoiced with him, humored him, harassed him with questions and even differed with him. It was in the presence of Fanny Burney and Hannah More and Mrs. Thrale that Johnson relaxed; at his second home with the Thrales that the stone figure showed a streak of wax. It is true that in Mrs. Thrale's "Anecdotes" we have "the aweful, melancholy, and venerable Johnson" in a more gracious, relaxed and unbuttoned mood than that in which he appears in Boswell's "Life" and that it was Hannah More who observed in him the mild radiance of the setting sun. The Doctor's letters to Mrs. Thrale, for example, show us the great man of the tavern as the tamed, playful bear. But Boswell's very awareness of the danger of over-emphasis was the cause of his protection; he felt that he did not have Johnson in the full gleam of every one of his facets. As early as 1776 he appealed to Mrs. Thrale for "a few of the admirable sayings" of Johnson which he knew she was collecting but could not then know she was to use herself, and he appealed to Fanny Burney for some of Johnson's "choice little notes," frankly acknowledging his problem: "we have seen him long enough upon stilts; I want to show him in a new light," Boswell told her. They were standing at the gate of the Queen's Lodge at Windsor, Miss Burney being at that time in servitude to Queen Charlotte, as second keeper of her robes. "Grave Sam, and great Sam, and solemn Sam, and learned Sam,—all these he has appeared over and over. Now I want to entwine a wreath of the graces across his brow; I want to show him as gay Sam, agreeable Sam, pleasant Sam; so you must help me with some of his beautiful billets to yourself." In his efforts to persuade her, he took out from his pockets proofs of his "Life" and read aloud from them, his curious conduct attracting a crowd and embarassing Miss Burney.

She was implacable, but although he appealed in vain, it is he who has placed Johnson between Falstaff and Gargantua, by giving full value to the caricatural side of Johnson, his bulk, his mannerisms, the details of his ugliness, the habits betokening indifferent breeding, his superstitions, his tyrannical assumption of the command of conversation, the numerous and various oddities this side insanity, the violence and the unexpectedness of his outbursts, the apparent capriciousness of his conduct and speech. Hawkins tells us: "In the talent of humour there hardly ever was his equal" and, again, that "of the talent of humour he had an almost enviable portion," but neglects to give us a single example. Boswell, on the other hand, aware as he is that he has given us rather too much of the philosopher and the moralist, presents us with an image of Johnson laughing like some jubilant,

Colossus-like figure of mythology—an image doubly delightful because it includes an onlooker who is blank with puzzlement, namely, Boswell. It was early in May, 1773. They had met in the Temple, in the lodgings of Robert Chambers, who had drawn up a will for a friend (identified as Langton) who was leaving his fortune to three sisters, to whom Johnson referred as dowdies. The playful mind of Ursa Major seized upon this will—of all things—as occasion for mirthfulness. He began laughing within the gates of the Temple and kept it up, amidst the splutter of his commentary, so that he had to hold on to one of the street posts for support, "and sent forth peals so loud, that in the silence of the night his voice seemed to resound from Temple-bar to Fleet-ditch." Later in the same year, during the Hebrides journey, he burst out in as unexpected a manner at the notion of owning an island in the Loch of Dunvegan, he seeing himself in his amused fancy advancing with his forces to take the Isle of Muck.

Boswell has been blamed for seizing upon the

abnormalities in Johnson, the peculiarities, rather than the normalities. Perhaps he has. But the presumption of integrity, in the minutest detail and in the largest generalization, is on his side. Boswell's Johnson is the only Johnson we have and admit, the descriptions of others serving but as footnotes to his. Wherever Boswell placed his emphasis there should it have been placed. If Boswell missed a slight shading of character, he did not miss the essential magnificent bulk. In whatever manner any other biographer, or diarist, crossed a *t* or dotted an *i* in Johnson's portrait, the emendation is of interest only as we can refer it to the basic portrait that Boswell gave us. If, for example, Johnson appeared somewhat more comical to Fanny Burney than he did to Boswell it is only when we superimpose such recollections as her's upon Boswell's massive portrait that the comic quality of the man appears the more vividly. Boswell's art is the better appreciated when we compare his biography with those others which, like moons, take their light from the sun that is Boswell's record. Boswell had biographical integrity and was justified of it. When Hannah More, at the time Boswell's "Tour to the Hebrides" was in press, begged that he would "mitigate" some of Johnson's "asperities," he answered "roughly": "He would not cut off his claws, nor make a tiger a cat to please anybody." Let others claim the doubtful honor of having pared the tiger's claws and turned his roar into a purr. For this was Boswell's intention, stated in the beginning of his work: "And he will be seen as he really was; for I profess to write, not his panegyrick, which must be all praise, but his Life, which, great and good as he was, must not be supposed to be entirely perfect. To be as he was, is indeed subject of panegyrick enough to any man in this state of being; but in every picture there should be shade as well as light, and when I delineate him without reserve, I do what he himself recommended, both by his precept and his example."

He told all he knew and did not spare himself in reportorial enterprise. He interviewed everybody who had touched Johnson's life in the smallest way. He wrote a multitude of letters in quest of data. No one who had ever crossed Johnson's path, even in the most casual way, was safe from pressing inquiry, for note, anecdote, recollection. From Frank Barber to the Bishop of Dromore he obtained what he could, from each according to his Johnsonian capacity, from Miss Porter at Lichfield, Dr. Taylor at Ashbourne, Hector at Birmingham, Adams at Oxford; from a dozen others, notably Langton, Reynolds and Beauclerk. He agreed most decidedly with the Rev. Dr. Maxwell of Falkland, Ireland, to whom he had appealed for Johnsonian data covering 1770, one of the years in which biographer and subject were parted and not a single note passed between them. "The very minutiae of such a character," wrote Maxwell, "must be interesting and may be compared to the filings of diamonds." Boswell himself refers to that talk as gold dust. Sir John Hawkins thought otherwise, or lacked the spirit of absorbed admiration and reverence that was Boswell's, and his industry. One cannot see the mean-spirited knight running over half of London to get one little date straight.

JOHNSON DRINKS SOME TEA

Rowlandson's caricature of Johnson being entertained by the Boswells at their Edinburgh home

Alone of all who have written of Johnson, Sir John had become acquainted with him during that middle period which came between utter poverty and independence, but did not choose to cast more than a casual beam of light into that period. Mrs. Thrale's reminiscences are good—after Boswell has corrected the inaccuracies—but they do not cast much light on those years of Johnson's about which we are most in the dark. Garrick came with Johnson to London but their ways parted almost immediately, re-joining when Garrick, largely for old time's sake, produced his teacher's tragedy, Irene. Nor did Johnson, when writing the lives of such authors as Savage, who shared with him the wretched plight preceding the dawn, choose to give us in writing any deep glimpses into his pre-pension period. Hawkins fails to come up to the opportunities extended to him by his acquaintance with Johnson. Boswell sometimes exhausted the patience of Johnson in attempting to exhaust the opportunities for Johnsoniana. Hawkins can do little more than deplore, in his puritanical manner, Johnson's association with

Savage; Boswell has no other concern than to extract information out of his conversational opportunities. He quotes a story Johnson told of Derrick—a poet who, Boswell had hoped, would introduce him to Johnson before Davies came to the breach—which story is symptomatic of the condition Johnson faced in his early days. "Sir, I honour Derrick for his presence of mind. One night when Floyd, another poor authour, was wandering about the streets in the night, he found Derrick fast asleep upon a bulk; upon being suddenly waked, Derrick started up, 'My dear Floyd, I am sorry to see you in this destitute state; will you go home with me to *my lodgings?*'" And this: "Soon after Savage's Life was published (in 1744) Mr. Harte dined wth Edward Cave, and occasionally praised it. Soon after, meeting him, Cave said, 'You made a man very happy t'other day!'—'How could that be?' said Harte; 'nobody was there but ourselves.' Cave answered, by reminding him that a plate of victuals was sent behind a screen, which was to Johnson, dressed so shabbily, that he did not choose to appear; but on hearing the conversation, he was highly delighted with the encomiums on his book." By means of which little anecdotes, which occurred when Boswell was not yet born, or was but an infant, he filled up the gaps a little in our knowledge of Johnson's early years.

In what ways did the cross-roads encounter of Johnson and Boswell influence the latter? Although we are compelled to revise our simple picture of a Boswell revolving only in the orbit of Johnson, it is undeniable that the task of keeping that record of his days and nights in which Johnson was so important a performer gave Boswell a job of more greatly sustained interest than any he ever had. No other job ever enlisted his interest and emotion to the same extent. Not his profession could give him so sustained a purpose, nor even his children. And once he was launched on the "Life," which was the fulfillment of the pledge he had made to do honor to Johnson's memory, his own life achieved at last a temporary discipline of purpose and was organized and integrated in a definite direction. No matter how scattered and volatile he was his mind must have returned to the heap of Johnsonian notes he had been accumulating as to a core of hidden strength, as a miser in moments of humiliation can draw power from the private knowledge of his hoard.

With the help of his notes Boswell relived the golden moments he had passed in Johnson's circle; defied, in Professor Tinker's phrase, the powers of oblivion, preserving Johnson as vivid and complete as he had been to him in the flesh, and later communicating the organized picture of that image for the world to share. As for Johnson's personal influence on Boswell, that is a little harder to weigh. Perhaps the moralist helped stiffen Boswell's spine. He was probably less of a sot while Johnson was around, although we should not wish Boswell to be other than he was, whatever he was. From a narrowly moral point of view it was better for Boswell that he attached himself to Johnson than to the Wilkes whom he thought "good without principle, and wicked without malevolence."

During the German tour when the rampant young Scotchman was contemplating the seduction of the Turkish woman who, by marriage, had become Madame de Froment, he talked morality instead and fancied himself a Johnson. There were at least two occasions during that part of the tour when he did not talk Morality, those in which participated the Prussian soldier's wife and the "Street Girl," not to mention his life in Edinburgh, preceding his marriage and thereafter. That Boswell would have been grateful for a moralistic rationalization of his sexual desires is shown in one of the talks he had with Rousseau, wherein he expressed a wish for thirty women. He had, however, the habit of suggesting the contrary of the principle in which he wished to be confirmed. He wished to be a Boswell of whom others might approve and was constantly adjusting himself to the presumed expectations of others. Although Boswell desired to be none other than Boswell, writing, " . . . and render him as fine a fellow as possible," he wished to be a Boswell of whom some other person, older and estimable, would approve. Johnson supplanted other models and became his chief influence to virtue.

If Johnson influenced Boswell for his good it was because Boswell was susceptible to that kind of influence, desired it and exposed himself to it. He was not influenced in despite of himself. He was a conventionally religious man whose impulses were inconveniently strong, who fought melancholy with conviviality, lapsed into conduct which his moral side could not allow to pass without reproach and found ever new reasons for melancholia and conviviality. He also shared Johnson's fear of death and there was undoubtedly a dash of fear in his morality. After meeting Johnson his vigilance redoubled. Writing to Lord Kames, Boswell said: "I beleive I told your Lordship before I left England that I had obtained the freindship of Mr. Samuel Johnson. I look upon this as the happiest incident in my life. The Conversation of that great and good man has formed me to manly Virtue, and kindled in my mind a generous ardour which I trust shall never be extinguished." He was, of course, prolific of intentions of virtue, and these indicated the variance of intention from practice, for his resolutions were somewhat more flamboyantly moral than his impulses permitted him to be. Boswell may be regarded as a trumped-up peace between two warring factions in himself. But to Sir David Dalrymple he wrote a report rather than a resolution: "I thank God that I have got acquainted with Mr. Johnson. He has done me infinite service. He has assisted me to obtain peace of mind. He has assisted me to become a rational Christian."

Whether Johnson's influence for good extended beyond his presence is debatable, in Boswell's case, although that influence may have deepened Boswell's sense of remorse upon visiting "the mansions of gross sensuality" without preventing those visits. It is even possible that Boswell's immorality was a bond and claim on Johnson's continuing interest. It is also possible that the uplifting pleasure Boswell derived from the making of resolutions was intensified by the regularity with which he broke them. Had he been a Catholic, he would have obtained from the confessional the same kind of purged relief which the composition of resolves gave him, and biography would then have been a little less burdened with accounts of his diverse affairs and their medical consequences. Sometime in 1773 Johnson decided to buy Boswell some books, and "I am to read more and drink less," he wrote to Temple. Quite a number of times did drink seriously betray him. During his courtship of Miss Blair, some years before, he had drunk her health so thoroughly that before the fumes had evaporated he had spent the night with a street woman and become infected. He later fell from a horse and injured himself, from the same cause, and about a dozen years after he wrote the note to Temple, he was found dead drunk on the pavement of Lancaster and was made to suffer humiliation in open court the next day.[1] Hannah More tells, in 1781, of

[1] Those who present the evidences of Boswell's indefatigable industry as proof that he could not have had margins of time and vitality for self-indulgences might better strengthen their admiration for Boswell by considering how hardy and gifted he must have been to have had time and

how "heartily disgusted" she was with "Mr. Boswell, who came upstairs [this was at Bishop Shipley's] after dinner much disordered with wine." Late in life he was often drunk and once, in 1793, he was attacked and robbed while drunk, being confined to bed by his injuries. Had Johnson made Boswell a better man, Mrs. Boswell might have been expected to show some gratitude. That both she and her father-in-law did not look favorably upon the bear who was leading their man is not absolute proof that Johnson left Boswell as he found him although it should be remembered that Mrs. Boswell, if not the Laird, relented and invited the bear to Scotland, about the time she sent him the orange marmalade, hoping, or knowing, that he would not come.

It would be foolish, however, to speculate on how much worse Boswell would have been had there been no Johnson. Before he had the hope

---

strength for self-indulgences, as well as the management—in later years—of an estate, the conduct of a law practice, the practice of politics, literature, journalism, social life and the maintenance of a far-flung correspondence.

of meeting Johnson, his mind was groping for a model. That Johnson became the model—supplanting a number of others, including his father, upon whom he had tentatively lighted—was to the greater ultimate advantage of the preceptor than the student. In that flamboyant style of his, he writes of Johnson to Wilkes: "My veneration and love for that illustrious philosopher is so great that I cannot promise to be allways free from some imitation of him. O John Wilkes . . . let Johnson teach thee the road to rational virtue and noble felicity." Others might have breathed the Johnsonian aether without becoming affected by it, but not Boswell. According to Miss Burney, Boswell imitated Johnson at least in the slovenly manner of his dress, as Goldsmith is said to have done. The more we realize his potentialities for independent greatness the greater is the implied tribute to Johnson for having kept him by him in a subordinate capacity. The fact argues a greatness in Johnson the man which has evaporated from the writings of Johnson. However volatile and gadding Boswell seemed he found in the task to which he set himself the great purpose of his life and in its completion the realization of at least one of his ambitions. By combating the superficial aspects of his character, he for a time denied their existence. In one of his most dejected letters to Temple, that of August 23, 1789, he wrote: "THE LIFE OF JOHNSON still keeps me up. I *must* bring that forth." The dominant ambition may have been literary fame, rather than service to Johnson, but whichever was dominant, both were satisfied to repletion.

When we consider how apparently inexhaustible in Johnsoniana and anecdotage is Boswell's "Life," we take it for granted that portrait painter and sitter were inseparable, from the year of their meeting until Johnson's death. Again, facts compel even greater admiration for the genius and the industry of Boswell. There were long periods of separation, apart from the years of Boswell's foreign study and travel, and even of the cessation of correspondence. The joint tour through Scotland which was so fertile in Johnsoniana was offset by many separations, separations rendered barren by the lack of correspondence. The richness of Boswell's gift to us in "The Life of Samuel Johnson" makes us unaware of the comparatively brief snatches of association on which it is based. For long periods Boswell was obliged to lead a more or less irksome existence away from the center of his universe. In the eyes of Boswell's family the force of the magnetic pull which Johnson exercised upon him across the vast expanse of Scottish moors and English meadows must have more than counterbalanced the hypothetical effects of his influence on Boswell's moral nature. But it was the pull of London that made Boswell restless in Edinburgh, London which to Boswell was "the great scene of ambition, instruction and amusement; a scene which was . . . comparatively speaking, a heaven upon earth," and, to Johnson, a place of which, if one tired one might as well cut his throat. Even when Johnson had passed away Boswell could not resist the lure of London.

Their first meeting occurred on Monday, May 16, 1763; their last, at Sir Joshua Reynolds's, on Wednesday, June 30, 1784. Johnson's last letter to Boswell was from Lichfield, dated Nov. 5, 1784. During this twenty-one-year period Boswell made no more than twelve visits to England, seeing Johnson 180 times, according to John Wilson Croker. Adding the days of the joint Scottish tour, they are believed to have spent 276 days together in all. On the basis of Dr. Birkbeck Hill's computation, the periods of time during which Johnson and Boswell were living near each other, if added together, would amount to about two years and on most days within that period it is likely that they did not see each other. Not only in 1770, but in 1782 also they did not see each other at all. During Johnson's last years they saw very little of each other and for the latter part of 1780 the record is eked out with the help of a friend. Because their destinies have been interwoven, we have imagined that their lives were. Boswell's genius and achievement loom the larger in the light of this knowledge.

The newly issued Boswell journals and letters strengthen this view, for they constitute, in Geoffrey Scott's words, "a constant reminder of how small a portion of Boswell's vivid and multifarious existence was associated with Johnson." Whenever it was that he made the decision to Boswellize, he took notes from the very beginning. Reporting their earliest jaunt, to Greenwich, Boswell apologizes for the paucity of his notes. "And here I am to mention with much regret, that my record of what he said is miserably scanty. I recollect with admiration an animating blaze of eloquence, which rouzed every intellectual power in me to the highest pitch, but must have dazzled me so much, that my memory could not preserve the substance of his discourse." And some twenty-five pages earlier he had written a similar apology: "In progress of time, when my mind was, as it were, strongly impregnated with the Johnsonian aether, I could, with much more facility and exactness, carry in my memory and commit to paper the exuberant variety of his wisdom and wit." Even during the Hebridean journey Boswell confessed remissness, on one occasion ignoring Johnson's talk to the company because it turned chiefly " on mechanicks, agriculture and such subjects, rather than on science and wit," and he upbraids himself for not spending more time with Johnson, now that he has him to himself—as a dog which has got hold of a large piece of meat which he has dragged to a corner.

Before he became impregnated with the Johnsonian aether he worked hard on his notes and, afterwards, he was obliged to use his ingenuity and industry to the utmost to obtain material on Johnson's early life and reports and letters from, and interviews with, others than Johnson to fill the gaps. On their return from Greenwich, on that first jaunt, Boswell shivers in the cold night air. " I was the more sensible of it having sat up all the night before, recollecting and writing in my journal what I thought worthy of preservation; an exertion, which, during the first part of my acquaintance with Johnson, I frequently made. I remember having sat up four nights in one week, without being much incommoded in the day time." Time and again he will apologize to the reader of his "Life" for neglecting to note various conversations.

He was compelled to develop his own method of shorthand, for use on the spot. He would make rough notes in Johnson's presence, or shortly thereafter, sometimes using torn scraps of paper. The first draft of the "Life" differed both from the published work and the notes from which it was constructed. When Paoli came to London he said that he had suspected Boswell of being a spy, for upon their first meeting Boswell had his tablets out and was writing. Boswell's note-taking fidelity sometimes was expressed in public in terms which might have embarrassed one thinner-skinned than Johnson. Mrs. Thrale, between whom and Boswell little love was lost, wrote of him without mentioning his name, as "sitting steadily down at the other end of the room to write at the moment what should be said in company, either *by* Dr. Johnson or *to* him." Robert Barclay had observed Boswell "lay down knife and fork and take out his tablets in order to register a good anecdote." Most of the time Johnson didn't mind; on several occasions he filled the blanks in Boswell's notes when the latter was uncertain of what he had said. Boswell had vanity of a kind, but not of the kind that would stand in the way of reportorial genius. "Desirous of calling Johnson forth to talk, and exercise his wit, though I should myself be the object of it, I resolutely ventured to undertake the defense of convivial indulgence in wine, though he was not to-night in the most genial humour." In his zeal to make his great diamond Johnson shed some precious filings he would ask questions time and again "with an assumed air of ignorance in order to incite Johnson to talk." Once the latter became angry at this perpetual questioning and cried out: "Don't you consider, Sir, that these are not the manners of a gentleman? I will not be baited with *what* and *why!* What is this? What is that? Why is a cow's tail long? Why is a fox's tail bushy?" "Sir," he said, with even greater exasperation on another occasion when he overheard him questioning Levett about him—"Sir, you have but two topics, yourself and me. I am sick of both." It is fortunate that Boswell rarely lost zest or zeal for the greater of those two topics. Another time he enraged Johnson by suggesting a bout of talk between him and Mrs. Catharine Macaulay, a " republican " friend of Johnson's and an historian. " Don't you know," he cried, " that it is very uncivil to *pit* two people against one another? " And on another occasion he must have intended a rebuff to Boswell when he said: " To be contradicted, in order to force you to talk, is mighty unpleasing. You *shine* indeed; but it is by being *ground.*" Combative as Johnson was, he did not always relish the gladiatorial role; for a change he preferred a quiet unobserved interchange of ideas between man and man. That conversation is happiest, he once had remarked, which is unmuddied by vanity or competition. From Dr. Burney's memoirs we learn how amazed was Boswell to discover one morning that the chair next to Johnson at the Thrale board had been given to her instead of to him, and that, nothing baffled, he took hold of another chair and placed it at the back of the Doctor's shoulder; and how he listened to none other as he waited for Johnson to speak, and the moment he did so: "His eyes goggled with eagerness; he leant his ear almost on the shoulder of the Doctor; and his mouth dropped open to catch every syllable that might be uttered: nay, he seemed not only to dread losing a word, but to be anxious not to miss a breathing; as if hoping from it, latently or mystically, some information." Referring to Sir Richard Musgrave, an Irish baronet, Miss Burney calls him "a caricature of Mr. Boswell, who is a caricature of all other of Dr. Johnson's admirers." In a marginal note on Boswell's "Life" Mrs. Thrale relates how Johnson came in one day and told her that he had been put to the question that morning and that he was now "panting for breath." "What sort of questions did he ask, I wonder?" "Why, one question was: 'Pray, Sir, can you tell me why an apple is round, and a pear pointed?' Would not such talk make a man hang himself?" On another occasion he asked Johnson what he would do if he were shut up in a tower with a baby.

Boswell's explanation is that Johnson usually put upon another the burden of initiating talk, Tom Tyers having likened him to a ghost who never speaks until he's spoken to. A suggestion made in a letter to Dr. James Beattie, professor of moral philosophy at Aberdeen, to whom Boswell had provided a letter of introduction to Johnson, takes cognizance of this Johnsonian peculiarity: "I would suggest to you that it may be necessary for you to exert yourself when with Mr. Johnson to lead him to talk of such subjects as are agreeable. You must not be discouraged though he should appear reserved and wanting in some of the commonplace modes of making a stranger easy." Boswell desired that he should be remembered for this service of "starting topics and making him pursue them," and he compared himself to a miller who throws in grist for the mill—Johnson—to grind, and added: "it requires, indeed, fertile minds to furnish materials for this mill. I regret whenever I see it unemployed." This is a fairer statement of the relationship than that of "Peter Pindar" who called Boswell a tomtit twirling on an eagle's back, or of Horace Walpole who referred to the pair as a mountebank and his zany. Boswell's virtues as an interviewer are the better appreciated when we contrast his effect on Johnson with that of Hawkins. Hawkins refers more than once to Johnson as mentally torpid and physically indolent and that he lacked the resources of the imaginative faculty with which to combat disease and melancholy. The point is that Hawkins left Johnson as he found him, inert; Boswell sought to stimulate him and did, however awkwardly and with whatever occasionally disastrous effects to himself.

In his introduction to the first edition of the "Life," Boswell hesitates to list the books consulted and the inquiries made lest he should be thought "ridiculously ostentatious," adding: "Let me only observe as a specimen of my trouble, that I have sometimes been obliged to run half over London, in order to fix a date correctly," and elsewhere: "Had his other friends been as diligent and ardent as I was, he might have been almost entirely preserved." And in recalling their last meeting at Sir Joshua's, he declares himself "vexed that a single word should have been forgotten." It was only late in their association that the industrious, meticulous and vigilant Boswell relaxed, neglecting, as Dr Birkbeck Hill points out, to squeeze any juice out of the occasion, dismissing a conversation indifferently or leaving it unrecorded. But Boswell had earned an occasional nod.

Not only was Boswell generally industrious in recording what happened; he was ingenious in directing, to the extent to which he was capable, the course of Johnson's life. He prompted many of the conversations that his note-books might be enriched, assuming, as before noted, an air of ignorance, and challenging Johnson's wit, though he should himself be the butt of it. Boswell's social curiosity was not delimited by position, prejudice or preconception. Large as was Johnson's humanity, it did not embrace Rousseau and Voltaire, whom he abominated, and Hume and the Abbé Raynal, upon whom he turned his back. Principles did not inconveniently stand between Boswell and men of eminence, whatever the reasons for their eminence. In a letter to Gray, one of the men of eminence whom Boswell did not know, although he had solicited an introduction to him from Temple, Walpole refers to the author of the "Account of Corsica" as "a strange being" who "has a rage of knowing anybody that ever was talked of. He forced himself upon me at Paris in spite of my teeth and my doors, and I see has given a foolish account of all he could pick up from me about King Theodore." In another letter Walpole refers to him as "that quintessence of busybodies." "I am really the *Great Man* now," Boswell wrote Temple in May, 1768, referring to the fact that he was visited in the forenoon by Hume and in the afternoon by Johnson, and had entertained, or was to entertain, at dinner, singly, or in groups, Sir John Pringle, Dr. Franklin, General Oglethorpe, Johnson, Garrick and Hume.

Heir to feudal estates, Tory and High Churchman though he was, Boswell manœuvred an introduction to Tom Paine, the hated republican and infidel. He contrived to be introduced to the notorious Mrs. Rudd, who saved her own neck in 1775 by turning King's evidence against the brothers Perreau, who were hanged for forgery. It appears that Boswell went about with her, for which his father threatened to disinherit him. With the help of Johnson, who furnished him with a note of introduction, he met John Wesley, to whom he was commended as a worthy and religious man. He rode with the condemned murderer, the Rev. Mr. Hackman, to Tyburn to see him executed and witnessed the hangings of many others to whom he had not been introduced. On one occasion he saw fifteen men hanged. Only George Selwyn, the wit, exceeded Boswell in his avidity for executions, one of the great public sports of the day.

At the time Boswell met Johnson he met also John Wilkes. Wilkes, popular idol and pamphleteer, had been thrown out of Parliament, but finally, won the right to sit in it. He was the man for whom London lighted bonfires when the Court of Appeals freed him from the Tower, and who, at one time, seemed destined to lead a rebellion in Lon-

WILKES AND LIBERTY

The famous satirical print of John Wilkes, made by William Hogarth

don against the authority of the King. During a visit to London Franklin observed that had Jack Wilkes's private conduct been as " exemplary " as that of George III, the throne might have been in greater hazard. Boswell preened himself almost as much on the acquaintance of Wilkes as on that of Johnson—and Johnson, naturally, hated Wilkes. He had written a pamphlet, "The False Alarm" (1770) in which he attempted to prove it an axiom of government that the expulsion of a member of Parliament was equivalent to exclusion. (Wilkes had been four times elected by Middlesex before he could sit in Parliament.) Wilkes responded with an open letter in which he referred to the pamphlet as "that effusion of servility and bombast." Some time before Wilkes had grazed the pride of Johnson in some comment on the Dictionary. It was not enough for Boswell that he had contrived to meet both men; he had to contrive that opposites though they were, they should meet each other, and the success which attended his efforts illustrates the manner in which he managed to stage-direct

Johnson's life now and then. To be sure, he was not insensible to the value of his own role. In introducing Wilkes to Johnson he sought to re-enact the part he had played about seven years before, when he had introduced General Paoli to Dr. Johnson, on which occasion he compared himself "to an isthmus which joins two great continents." [He had dwelt on the plan of bringing Voltaire and Rousseau together.] The difference between Johnson and Wilkes is illustrated by the latter's remark to Boswell: "What! does *he* talk of liberty? *Liberty* is as ridiculous in *his* mouth as *Religion* in *mine*."

Very ingeniously he obtained Johnson's consent to attend a dinner that the booksellers Dilly were to give on Wednesday, May 15, 1776, obtaining that consent before informing him that Jack Wilkes *might* be there, playing successfully on Johnson's contrariness. And when Johnson was in the coach on the way to the Dillys's, Boswell exulted "as much as a fortune hunter who has got an heiress into a post-chaise with him to set out for Gretna Green." Not only was Jack Wilkes there, but present also was Mr. Arthur Lee, who "was not only a *patriot* but an *American*," and who was to serve the United States as minister to Spain. The year, recall, was 1776. Johnson was rabidly anti-American, having attempted, the year before, to throttle the American cause with a pamphlet called "Taxation no Tyranny," (which John Wesley, after abridging and re-titling, had issued under his own name) and as early as 1769, discussing the colonists, he had said to Dr. John Campbell: "Sir, they are a race of convicts, and ought to be thankful for anything we allow them short of hanging." The name American always made him lose his head, breathe fire and fury and roar tremendous volleys—"Rascals—Robbers—Pirates." He declared himself quite ready to love anybody but an American, and knew precisely how the colonists might be subjugated. One of his proposals called for the destruction of the house of every American who refused to allow soldiers to be quartered in it.

Mr. Wilkes sat himself next to Johnson and began helping him to some cuts of veal. Butter wouldn't melt in Jack Wilkes's mouth. Boswell's gleeful picture of the scene clearly indicates the rich personal charm of Wilkes and deepens the regret that the young Scotchman could not have served Wilkes as well as Johnson. "Pray, give me leave, Sir:—It is better here—A little of the brown—Some fat, Sir—A little of the stuffing—Some gravy—Let me have the pleasure of giving you some butter—Allow me to recommend a squeeze of the orange;—or the lemon, perhaps, may have some zest." "Sir, Sir, I am obliged to you, Sir," cried Johnson, bowing, and turning his head to him with a look for some time of 'surly virtue,' but, in a short while, of complacency." Before the night was over, they had got together on their common prejudice against the Scotch, with Boswell as butt. Nevertheless, the stage-manager in Boswell was tickled beyond words. Five years later, at another dinner at the Dillys', Boswell had the pleasure of surprising the old enemies in a tête-á-tête discussion of the quarrel between George II and the King of Prussia. In one little enterprise Boswell did fail: he could not bring Johnson to Wilkes's house for dinner.

Boswell contrived the journey to the north and one to the Midlands, obtained the account of Johnson's interview with the king, his undeveloped notes on the French trip with the Thrales, scraps of observation notable for their revelation of Johnson's provincialism; and the famous letter to Lord Chesterfield dispensing with His Lordship's offer of patronage for the Dictionary and containing this sardonic judgment on patrons: "Is not a Patron, my Lord, one who looks with unconcern on a man struggling for life in the water, and, when he has reached ground, encumber him with help?" And this mixture of pathos and pride: "The notice which you have been pleased to take of my labours, had it been early, had been kind; but it has been delayed until I am indifferent, and cannot enjoy it; till I am solitary and cannot impart it; till I am known, and do not want it."

Johnson wrote this letter but, for Boswell, it might have been swallowed by oblivion. However, we have this definition of patron in his Dictionary: "One who countenances, supports or protects. Commonly a wretch who supports with insolence and is paid with flattery." We recall Johnson's irritation when he heard Boswell asking Levett questions about himself. An incident reported in the "Memoirs of Thomas Holcroft," multiplied several hundreds of times, may give us a notion of the almost superhuman industry which Boswell applied to his task. The incident gives support to the thesis that only a man in whom there was a streak of contemptibleness could have run the risk of humiliation so often as did Boswell. The author of the "Memoirs" got the story from Mauritius Lowe, the painter, obviously a poor and humble man, who had applied to Johnson to write some letters for him, and these were not the only begging letters Johnson wrote for him. As he was writing Boswell came in and as Lowe, letters in his hand, was leaving the room, Boswell followed. Boswell's attention and solicitude quite surprised Lowe. The purpose of Mr. Boswell's attention was to persuade Lowe to permit him to see what Johnson had written for him; "everything from that hand, you know, is so inestimable." It is private, but Mr. Lowe is persuaded to hand it over. Boswell reads, he begs for the privilege of copying, suggesting Peele's Coffee House as the nearest suitable place. "I was so overcome by this sudden familiarity and condescension, accompanied by bows and grimaces, I had no power to refuse. We went to the coffee-house. My letter was presently transcribed, and as soon as he had put his document in his pocket Mr. Boswell walked away as erect and as proud as half an hour before. I ever after was unnoticed. Nay, I am not certain," added he sarcastically, "whether the Scotchman did not leave me, poor as he knew I was, to pay for my own dish of coffee." Internal evidence in the "Life" indicates that Johnson wrote two letters on that day, one to Sir Joshua and one to Mr. Barry to the end that a painting of Mr. Lowe's which had been rejected, be received into the exhibition of the Royal Academy. Johnson's intercession succeeded in obtaining a revocation of the first decision. However, it was hung in an empty room and was, according to one observer, " execrable beyond belief."

CHAPTER FIVE

"By All Tokens Samuel Johnson Was . . ."

BY all tokens Samuel Johnson was destined for a life of solitude. That he should survive as the prince of good company strikes one as an especially paradoxical joke on the part of Destiny. The scrofulous taint which disfigured his features, his hypochondria, the repulsiveness of his table manners and his indifference to clean linen, the variety of his odd habits betokening inclination toward insanity—Hogarth observing the antics of a strange person in Richardson's shop supposed him to be an "ideot"—and the irascibility of that "ideot's" temper—all these characteristics, it would seem, would tend inevitably to exclude even the gifted person oppressed by them from polite society, even polite male society, although male table manners in the eighteenth century were none too finical. But as the grandeur of Garrick's acting had the power to make his audiences forget his inadequate stature for heroic roles, so could the mind of Samuel Johnson, once launched in talk, make those who heard him forgetful of his body and of its strange movements and grimaces. Ozias Humphry, who has left us a number of excellent portraits of the Johnsonian school, visiting his most distinguished sitter at Inner Temple Lane in 1764, testified both to the idiocy of his manner and the perfection of his speech. He thought Johnson a madman " as he sat waving over his breakfast," but then he spoke and " everything he says is as correct as a second edition." At the beginning Boswell almost despaired of conveying on paper the force of Johnson's talk, so magnificent was it. " Every sentence is an essay," exclaimed one traveling companion, in the Oxford post coach, and once when Boswell had drawn him out to discuss Aristotle's theory in the " Art of Poetry," of the purging of the passions through terror and pity, one Joseph Cradock, who was present, whispered, "O that his words were written in a book!" They were, decidedly.

The figure of Johnson stands out the more memorably by virtue of the fact that it dominated a group which included Goldsmith, Burke, Gibbon, Reynolds, Garrick, Adam Smith, Bishop Percy, John Wilkes, and Dr. Burney, to mention only those whose names have survived out of the several scores of notable and interesting contemporaries. And these few names only feebly suggest the richness and variety of the Johnsonian circle, the intrinsic richness of personality not always being commensurate with posthumous reputation, or survival value. Adam Smith, however, can hardly be claimed as a 100 percent Johnsonian, for although a member of The Club he had little in common with Johnson, except a sharp difference of opinion on religion. Of this difference Boswell, in a letter, supplies a hint when he suggests that Johnson knock together the heads of those two infidels—Hume and Smith. But there was a bond. Smith praised the Dictionary in the Edinburgh Review and called the Preface in Johnson's edition of Shakespeare "the most manly piece of criticism that was ever published in any country."

Of Joseph Baretti, an Italian, one of the group, we might have known more had not a violent antagonism arisen between him and Boswell—unfortunately, a sometimes sufficient reason for the subordination, in Boswell's story, of a member of the Johnson circle Baretti had a rich, although a violent and quarrelsome, personality. He wrote various volumes, an English-Italian Dictionary, stabbed a man to death in the Haymarket in self-defense, was acquitted at the Old Bailey, partly on the character testimony of Burke, Garrick and Johnson, was tutor to the Thrale children and left us some pungent comment on Johnson and the Thrale circle. He was so vicious, treacherous and scheming, even attempting to set servants and children against the Thrales, that others than Boswell had reason to regret that he was not hanged. Persistence in a lie cost Baretti permanent estrangement from Johnson. Then there were Bennet Langton and Topham Beauclerk; the former distinguished for his piety, goodness, domesticity and scholarship in Greek literature; the latter, the great-grandson of Nell Gwynn and Charles II, by his amours, his good taste and the charm and effortlessness of his wit.

There was Thrale, next to the Crown, Johnson's chief single benefactor, General Oglethorpe and General Paoli, and numerous members of the nobility; politicians, divines—with which class Johnson was on excellent terms, including the too punctual Wesley who would leave off talk with Johnson to go off to some old women—and, inevitably, booksellers. He numbered the brilliant Colonel Forrester of the Guards and Lord Thurlow, the Lord Chancellor, among his friends. He was present at the gay parties given by the famous bluestocking Mrs. Vesey, whose husband was a member of the Club, and he knew his way about in other salons, so that we must qualify the simple picture of Johnson as some filthy Cyclops. Among his biographers and the recorders of Johnsonisms there were, in addition to Boswell, Mrs. Thrale-Piozzi and Sir John Hawkins, his official biographer, Tom Tyers and Arthur Murphy. It was Murphy, actor, dramatist and journalist and one of the most loveable of the Johnson circle, who brought Johnson the offer of a pension from the government and who introduced him to the Thrale household. His biographical essay appeared in connection with a twelve-volume edition of Johnson's works which came out in 1792. Jonathan Tyers, Tom's father, founded the famous Vauxhall Gardens. The women of the Johnson circle included, besides the trying females to whom his house was shelter, and the mistress of the Thrale household, Fanny Burney, Hannah More, Elizabeth Carter and Mrs. Charlotte Lennox. He " dined one day with the beautiful, gay and fascinating Lady Craven, and the next with the good Mrs. Gardiner, the tallow-chandler, on Snow Hill." The men who gathered about Johnson put in the shade the group which, in the proceding literary reign, assembled under the banner of the great Scriblerus Club, of which some of the chief figures were Gay, Pope, Swift, Arbuthnot and Bolingbroke, and the chief purposes of which were to help men of wit and confound men of Whiggery.

It is a tribute to the greatness of Johnson that he loved a wider variety of human beings than the strict interpretation of his moral principles would have allowed, his humanity superseding even his intellectual limitations, as his greatness supersedes those limitations, appealing as profoundly to those who do not share his opinions as to those who do. Reynolds was an artist, Burney a musician, Beauclerk somewhat of a profligate; Johnson loved them all, although ignorant of art, indifferent to music, an enemy to profligacy. We have seen how he was won over by the charm of Wilkes. By the rule of consistency, he, the Tory, should have fought Burke, the Whig, but it was Burke who spoke up in the House of Commons when the continuance of the old bear's pension seemed momentarily threatened. Dominating as he was by temperament, and persuaded as he was that his way to salvation, political and theological, was the right way, life nevertheless taught him that men made in other moulds than those of which he approved, must be lived with. "Dr. Johnson," Boswell tells us, "was willing to take men as they are, imperfect and with a mixture of good and bad qualities."

During the early part of Boswell and Johnson's tour of Scotland, the fancy struck the younger man that were the members of The Club exported to St. Andrews they would constitute a rather admirable faculty which would attract "a wonderful concourse of students." Johnson joined in the game of apportioning departments of learning to the members. The passage is in Boswell's "Journal" of the tour and gives an excellent idea of the variety of scholarship and the wealth of information from which the members must have drawn for the purposes of talk and debate:

"I was to teach Civil and Scotch law; Burke, politicks and eloquence; Garrick, the art of publick speaking; Langton was to be our Grecian, Colman our Latin professor; Nugent to teach physick; Lord Charlemont, modern history; Beauclerk, natural philosophy; Vesey, Irish antiquities, or Celtick learning; Jones, Oriental learning; Goldsmith, poetry and ancient history;

DR. JOHNSON ON TOUR

In the travelling dress he wore on his Scottish journey. Drawn from life and engraved by T. Trotter

Chamier, commercial politicks; Reynolds, painting, and the arts which have beauty for their object; Chambers, the law of England. Dr. Johnson at first said, "I'll trust theology to nobody but myself." But upon due consideration, that Percy is a clergyman, it was agreed that Percy should teach practical divinity and British antiquities; Dr. Johnson himself, logic, metaphysicks, and scholastick divinity."

Johnson was the elder of the majority of men and women whose names are linked with his. Garrick, to whom he stood in the relation of teacher at Edial, was, strangely enough, closest to him in age, being only eight years younger. Beauclerk and Langton were about thirty years younger and even Reynolds, whose kindness and wisdom shine throughout Boswell's record, and who, in manner, sometimes gave evidence of greater dignity than Johnson had, was fourteen years Johnson's junior, a tyro in art when Johnson already had made a name for himself in letters. Goldsmith, whom Reynolds encouraged although the material seemed most unpromising, was only five years younger than the painter.

Burke was only thirty-five at the organization of The Club in 1764, and Boswell, it will be recalled, was only twenty-two when, in the previous year, he met Johnson, a sage of fifty-four. Johnson compelled The Club to accept Boswell by threatening to black-ball every other man's candidate were Boswell rejected.[1] But "now you are in, none of them are sorry." But Boswell had to cool his heels for almost ten years before he was accepted and even Garrick had to take his time.

Gibbon had not published even the first volume of his History; and was twenty-eight years junior to the doughty moralist, whose judgments must sometimes have brought the characteristic sneer to his face. Even Thomas Sheridan, the father of Richard Brinsley, was eighteen years younger than Johnson. The elder Sheridan, it will be remembered, was the first to whom Boswell turned in his quest for an introduction to Johnson. Arthur Murphy was eighteen years younger than Johnson and Dr. Burney,

[1] Since one blackball was enough to exclude a candidate, this was a most effective threat.

the father of Fanny, was seventeen years his junior, while the precocious Fanny was young enough not merely to be the gruff old man's daughter, but even his grand-daughter, he being forty-three years her senior. Thus Johnson ruled over a generation of which his own children—had he had any—might have been a part. "Sir," he said to Boswell, in the early stage of their friendship, "I love the acquaintance of young people; because, in the first place, I don't like to think of myself growing old. In the next place, young acquaintances must last longest, if they do last; and then, Sir, young men have more virtue than old men; they have more generous sentiments in every respect."

And at least once these young men of his showed a fear of him which speaks volumes for his influence in his own time. Goldsmith had died and Johnson had written a Latin epitaph for his monument in Westminster Abbey. It occurred to some friends and acquaintances of Goldsmith, gathered at dinner at Reynolds's, that some changes might be made, including the rewriting of the epitaph into English. "But," as Sir William Forbes wrote Boswell, "who should have the courage to propose them to him?" Not one of the little mice dared go out and bell the cat, so they got up a round robin that Johnson should not know who was the ringleader of the conspiracy. Edmund Burke and Reynolds were among the signers, Bennet Langton refusing to affix his name, not out of fear but because he agreed with Johnson. Reynolds bore the petition to the monarch of letters and heard from him the decision that "he would never consent to disgrace the walls of Westminster Abbey with an English inscription" and the Latin inscription was engraved.[2] Cowper, writing to the Rev. John Newton, who had suggested putting a copy of the poet's "Moral Satires" in the doctor's way, expressed the fear that a blasting word from Johnson would spoil the sale, but should he be pleased, "I shall have engaged on my side one of the best

[2] It was late in Johnson's life that the character of The Club became diluted by the infusion of members not of the Johnsonian school, and he himself became less diligent in attendance and indifferent as to who might become members of it.

trumpeters in the kingdom." Langton, writing to Boswell, described an evening at Mr. Vesey's, where the company, which included Lords and Duchesses ranged itself, four or five deep, around the seated Johnson, with curiosity to see and to hear. (Vesey was the Celtic scholar whose wife was a distinguished bluestocking of the time and gave famous parties.) It should be remarked, however, that these members of the nobility regarded Johnson as a curiosity rather than as a fellow-equal, and there was a large group among the nobility, the wits and the fashionables, who lived a life apart from, and uninfluenced by, the Johnsonians.

Chief among these was Horace Walpole, who became the fourth earl of Orford, son of the great politician, Robert Walpole, [" Bob the poet's foe "] whose services for the House of Hanover had earned for that somewhat dilettante and finicky son of his a cultured, cushioned ease. At Strawberry Hill, his small-scale, filigree Gothic castle, into which he escaped from a social and political scene too troubling to participate in, he indulged to the utmost his flair for collecting, gathering together prints, paintings, bas-reliefs, enamels, reliquaries, odds and ends of precious antiques, including an example of Cellini's workmanship and the spurs King William wore at the Battle of the Boyne. He had also a rare collection of books, indulged himself in the hobby of operating a private press, from which he printed diverse items for the delectation of his friends. He was himself an author, his "Castle of Otranto" inaugurating the Gothic vogue in fiction, a vogue which Scott brought to its height with his medieval romances. He served in the House of Commons, but with none of that zest which he devoted to his private pursuits, nor did he ever take his seat in the House of Lords. It is in his letters that we have Horace Walpole in his most brilliant and most sustained expression—as keen an observer and as polished a stylist as the practitioners of the gentlest art can claim. But there was nothing gentle in his remarks on Johnson and his 'gang' in his letters and elsewhere. The over-chiselled Walpole refers to the rough-hewn massive sculpture of Johnson as "a brute," "a renegade," "an old decrepit hireling," "an odious and mean character," "an unfortunate monster trusting to his helpless deformity for indemnity for any impertinence that his arrogance suggests." When, at the Royal Academy, Reynolds offered to introduce Johnson to Walpole, the latter put his foot down: "No, Sir Joshua . . . You shall *not* present Dr. Johnson to me," which was, after all, treating Johnson to his own medicine. It was a limitation in each of these men that neither liked the other, and it was characteristic that the poodle should bark more vigorously about it than the mastiff.

"I never courted the great," Johnson could truly say, and Chesterfield could substantiate the statement; "they sent for me; but I think they now give me up. They are satisfied, they have seen enough of me." Upon Boswell demurring, Johnson adds: "No, Sir; great lords and great ladies don't love to have their mouths stopped."[3]

[3] The names of men of title are proportionately frequent in the list of these members of The Club who did not attend Johnson's funeral; Sir Charles Bunbury was the only mem-

"No man who ever lived by literature," he said on another occasion, "has lived more independently than I have done."

Boswell indicates enough of the charm of Beauclerk and of the power in conversation of Burke to make us regret that his own power fell short of including them in his rich narrative, or else that there were not enough Boswells to go around. Professor Tinker makes the point that had Boswell been less indifferent to mere pyrotechnical displays, of epigram and bon mot, such as the conversation of Garrick, the younger Sheridan and Beauclerk abounded in, he might have enriched his narrative. From Johnson's own admission Beauclerk could not only say good things, but—"No man ever was so free, when he was going to say a good thing, from a *look* that expressed that it was coming; or when he said it, from a look that expressed that it had come." Only Beauclerk could be consistently insolent to Johnson without forfeiting his com-

---

ber of hereditary title who was present. It is somewhat of a shock to see the name of Boswell on the list of the absent, but he was in Scotland at the time.

pany. When he heard of Johnson's pension he had the face to say to him: "I hope you'll now purge and live cleanly, like a gentleman." When Johnson intimated that Beauclerk might learn to command his temper, the young dandy could say: "I should learn of *you,* Sir." Once, when Boswell sought to defend someone against Beauclerk by calling him "a man of good principles," "Beau" responded, "then he does not wear them out in practice." Johnson asserted that he envied Beauclerk for his talents more than any other man. Beauclerk was as much the antithesis of Langton as he was of Johnson; Langton, who topped by a head every other member of The Club; pious, scholarly, dutiful family man of whom Johnson's only complaint was that he had his children too much about him.

Langton and Beauclerk were linked as students at Oxford and there it was that they first learned to admire the writings of Johnson. Their acquaintance with Johnson dates from 1752 when they first met, much to their surprise, the author they had admired. The most charming episode which Boswell reports in the relationship of this seemingly ill-assorted trio is that of a night in 1752 when Langton and Beauclerk having supped together at a London tavern and having sat until 3 in the morning thought to get Johnson to go with them on a "ramble." In answer to their knock on his door he appeared in his shirt, with a little black wig on top of his head and a poker in his hand, thinking that burglars had aroused him, but seeing who they were and hearing what their mission was, he replied jovially: "What is it, you dogs! I'll have a frisk with you." They went to Covent Garden where the green-grocers and fruiterers were arranging their "goods" but these worthies stared so at Johnson in his awkward attempt to help them that he gave it up. They went to a tavern, walked down to the Thames, took a boat to Billingsgate and persevered in dissipation for some time after Langton, who had an engagement to breakfast with some ladies, left them. Of his "Lanky" Johnson could say: "I know not who will go to Heaven if Langton does not." Like Fox and

Gibbon, Langton was a listener, rather than disputant, but, unlike them, not because he differed. But for one quarrel on religion, which ruffled a friendship of more than twenty years' standing, the relations between Langton and Johnson were as perfect as relations with Johnson could be.

After Johnson, the role of debater was played best by Burke. So restless was the great Parliamentary debater that, according to Johnson, were someone speaking at one end of the table, he would speak to someone else at the other. According to Reynolds, Burke could say in one evening ten things of such superlative wit that any one of them could keep the reputation of another man for a whole year. Burke's presence seemed to act as a challenge on Johnson and although Burke could say, after a bout of talk on Johnson's part, "It is enough for me to have rung the bell to him," Johnson once, when ill, hearing the name of Burke, burst out: "That fellow calls forth all my powers. Were I to see Burke now it would kill me." Langton told Boswell of a magnificent bout between Johnson and Burke on the classic poets, Johnson for

Homer, Burke for Virgil, but that is all we know of the occasion. It was on another occasion when the means for defending Baretti on the murder charge were being considered that Johnson, reproved for the warmth of his dialectic, said: "It may be so, for Burke and I should have been of one opinion if we had had no audience." Burke apparently was less eager for victory in talk than was Johnson—after all, Burke had the House of Commons to play in—and far less envious than Goldsmith has been represented as being of the man upon whom attention was centered.

If we are to believe Boswell, Goldsmith haunted the company of Johnson that he might learn to emulate him in the domination of a room, was hurt on those occasions when he was entirely overshadowed or overlooked and was envious of the attention Johnson attracted, at times seeking to deprecate him. Goldsmith was so unprepossessing in his appearance that he gave the impression of being a "low mechanick" rather than an author. Johnson objected that Goldsmith talked for effect, but

EDMUND BURKE IN ACTION

Contemporary caricature of Burke on the floor of the House of Commons

that the effect of his conversation was to make people doubt that he was as great as his writings. "No man," observed Johnson, "was more foolish when he had not a pen in his hand, or more wise when he had." And once he arose in his might at Reynolds's table to confound certain gentlemen who were attempting to deprecate Goldsmith as a writer. "If nobody was suffered to abuse poor Goldy, but those who could write as well, he would have few censors." At least one biographer of Goldsmith has declared that Boswell grossly libelled Goldsmith, misunderstood or misrepresented the nature of Goldsmith's Irish humor, intrigued to foment trouble between Goldsmith and Johnson and deprecated Goldsmith's independent achievements, trying to account for them on the ground of Johnson's assistance. Boswell intrigued, according to this ingenious explanation, because he feared that Goldsmith might be appointed Johnson's biographer and be given the raw materials for such a Life. The success of his intrigue is supposed to have been marked in Johnson's answer to Mrs.

Thrale, when she suggested that Goldsmith would serve well as a biographer: "The dog would write it best, to be sure, but his particular malice towards me, and general disregard for truth, would make the book useless to all, and injurious to my character." This fear was absurd, for malice was not in Goldsmith's veins—not as a writer, anyway. But had Boswell's portrait been unlike that drawn by any other contemporary the defenders of Goldsmith would have had more cause to berate Boswell. There is Hawkins who not only put down Goldsmith as "this idiot in the affairs of the world"—an unintended compliment, from Hawkins—but calls him rude and absurd, an imitator of Johnson's mode of conversation, and envious of praise bestowed on Dr. Major, to whom Goldsmith played the role of Dr. Minor. What Boswell and Hawkins may not have remarked was that Goldsmith was probably expressing, in disguised forms, a sense of irritation at the indifferent reception his works were receiving. Dr. Hill has justly applied to Goldsmith Johnson's excuse for vanity in the poet Savage: "Vanity may surely be readily pardoned in him to whom life afforded no other comforts than barren praises, and the consciousness of deserving them."[4] And what correspondence between Goldsmith and Boswell we have—slight as it is—is sufficient indication that their relations were cordial, or at least be-

[4] Goldsmith's improvidence and poverty are illustrated in the famous anecdote out of Boswell's "Life," in which Johnson saves Goldsmith from his landlady's bailiff by obtaining an advance of 60 pounds on "The Vicar of Wakefield." The incident, which occurred in 1764, is thus told by Boswell, in Johnson's words:

"I received one morning a message from poor Goldsmith that he was in great distress, and as it was not in his power to come to me, begging that I would come to him as soon as possible. I sent him a guinea, and promised to come to him directly. I accordingly went as soon as I was drest, and found that his landlady had arrested him for his rent, at which he was in a violent passion. I perceived that he had already changed my guinea, and had got a bottle of Madeira and a glass before him. I put the cork into the bottle, desired he would be calm, and began to talk to him of the means by which he might be extricated. He then told me that he had a novel ready for the press, which he produced for me. I looked into it, and saw its merit; told the landlady I should soon return, and having gone to a bookseller, sold it for sixty pounds. I brought Goldsmith the money, and he discharged his rent, not without berating his landlady for having used him so ill."

came so after Boswell, following the success of "She Stoops to Conquer," reached the conclusion that Goldsmith was an autonomous celebrity. Yet, if Boswell had had no other cause for gratitude to Goldsmith than the introduction to Sir Joshua Reynolds that cause would have been sufficient to assure justice, if not gratitude, at Boswell's hands. In one of his political-journalistic writings, Boswell refers to the acquaintance of Sir Joshua as that "jewel of the finest water" that Goldsmith gave him.

But the artist first met Johnson, as had the musician, Burney, in his writings. Dr. Burney's first letter to Johnson consisted of an inquiry as to how he might order six copies of the English Dictionary, an inquiry of the kind which is the surest passage to an author's heart. Later, when Burney had established himself in London, Johnson was sometimes a guest at the musicales he gave at his house in St. Martin's Street and whenever Burney visited Streatham he could be counted on to stay up and engage Johnson in post-midnight chat. Reynolds became acquainted with Johnson on that memorable day when "standing with his arm leaning against a chimney-piece" he began reading the anonymous Life of Savage and read on without a stop until his arm had become numbed. Their first physical meeting was at the Misses Cotterells, daughters of Admiral Cotterell. It was an apparently callous, but truly wise, remark of Reynolds's that attracted Johnson. "The ladies were regretting the death of a friend to whom they owed great obligations," and Reynolds then remarked: "You have, however, the comfort of being relieved from a burthen of gratitude."

Reynolds was always a most gracious host and under the roof of his house in Leicester Fields gathered the intelligence, the wit and the genius of London—"temporal and spiritual peers, physicians, lawyers, actors and musicians composed the motley group"—for those Bohemian dinners at which there were often more guests than knives and forks. It was at that house that Boswell and Johnson met for that last time, at dinner. Johnson would have preferred Reynolds to have exercised more discrimination, in favor of those who shared Johnsonian principles, yet Reynolds was as much under Johnson's domination as the Doctor could have wished. Writing of those "Discourses" on art which he had already delivered, Reynolds asserted: "Whatever merit they may have must be imputed, in a great measure, to the education I may be said to have had under Dr. Johnson." And in a letter he paid Johnson this tribute: "He may be said to have formed my mind, and to have brushed from it a great deal of rubbish." Reynolds was probably the only man who could effectively rebuke Johnson for his violence and rudeness in speech and Boswell reports at least one reproof which was so gentle and to such point that it brought the blush to Johnson's cheek. "There goes a man not to be spoiled by prosperity," Johnson once said of the painter as the latter was leaving a room. He also declared of him that he was so invulnerable that if you should quarrel with him, you would lack any handle for abuse. Johnsonians are forever indebted to Sir Joshua, not only for the portraits but for the anecdotes which he fed Boswell and it was to Reynolds that Boswell dedicated the

"Life." Reynolds gave Boswell the portrait of Johnson which was used as frontispiece to the "Life" and it hung at Auchinleck until Boswell's eldest son, ashamed of his father's subservience to Johnson, removed it from the sitting room and sent it to the attic.

Although the tavern was Johnson's favorite haunt he was no misogynist. To his mother and his wife he was devotion; he suffered keenly from the bad tempers of the women to whom he gave shelter. He doted on Fanny Burney, who, in return, aped the Johnsonian style and spoiled whatever style she might have claimed as her own. He was as gracious as he could be to Mrs. Thrale, whom he called "Mistress" and who, upon her husband's death, paid him back for the allegiance towards him which her masterful husband had virtually enforced. Once, expressing some unflattering verdict on women, he excepted Mrs. Thrale and Miss Burney, for "they are goddesses." Nothing pleased the latter so much as Johnson's praise for her first novel, "Evelina," and on the day before his death she almost cried her eyes out, waiting on the stairs leading to his bedroom for the summons that never came. And Hannah More was almost as pleased at the flattering attentions which Johnson paid her as a minor female American poet might be at the notice of a lecturing English author, and she fed him flattery to the gorging point. Johnson was one of the most devoted friends of Mrs. Charlotte Lennox, a minor novelist of whom we no longer hear. It was he who wrote some of her dedications, reviewed her books, published Proposals for a collected edition of that lady's works, and pushed and puffed her in other ways because he believed in her.

Hawkins describes a celebration Johnson staged for her in 1751 on the occasion of the appearance of her first novel, "The Life of Harriet Stuart." The party was held at the Devil Tavern between Temple Gate and Temple Bar, that tavern over whose floor had trod an earlier Jonson, and Swift and Addison and Steele. The celebration began at eight in the evening and ended at eight in the morning, long before which time most of the twenty guests were dead from lack of sleep. Although Johnson had nothing stronger than lemonade, his "face shone with meridian splendor." It was he who upon the brow of Mrs. Lennox placed the crown of laurel, which has withered in more than one sense. No doubt Johnson would have seized a lesser occasion for as ebullient an outburst. He loved company, he loved talk, he loved the tavern and a party dominated by Johnson embraced the three elements. He who could give a passing Thames boatman this coup: "Sir, your wife, *under pretence of keeping a bawdy-house*, is a receiver of stolen goods," could also deliver this graceful compliment to the great Mrs. Siddons, who, when calling upon him, found no chair ready: "Madam, you who so often occasion a want of seats to other people, will the more readily excuse the want of one yourself."

CHAPTER SIX

"Samuel Johnson Was Born In . . ."

SAMUEL JOHNSON was born in Lichfield, Staffordshire, Sept. 18, 1709, the son of a poor bookseller and magistrate, Michael Johnson, from whom he inherited his scrofulous taint, a "vile melancholy," his inability to get the best of a bargain, and upon his death in 1731, no more than twenty pounds. His father was 53 years of age, his mother 37, at his birth, and Johnson's dislike of parents who would insist on showing off their children originated in the distress he suffered at the awkward pride which his father had in him. So much did he fear being shown off that he would sometimes seek refuge up a tree. He was very much alone and the surprising habit of his maturity of muttering to himself even when in company must have originated on his lonely peregrinations around Lichfield; Stourbridge, where also he went to school, and at Oxford. A Lichfield schoolmate testified to the early origin of that habit. Even when not alone, he was more engaged in talking to himself than in paying attention to his youthful companions. But when he did, he dominated, then, as later, for some of his schoolmates used to call to carry him to school. But his home life was not happy, his father's poverty being one cause, and many years later, he was to refer, with a slight pang, to the pleasant harmony of the Burney home. "I who have no sisters nor brothers, look with some degree of innocent envy on those who may be said to be born to friends," he wrote, at the age of forty-nine, in a letter to Langton. Between Samuel and his younger brother Nathanael, not much love was lost. (The latter died in 1737, at the age of twenty-five.) Lacking real brothers and sisters, young Samuel made books both brother and sister. Looking for some apples one day, young Samuel discovered Petrarch and devoured him instead.

However unfortunate may have been the inheritance he received from his father, it did include the use of a collection of books. On being admitted to Oxford, the new gawk of a scholar struck into the middle of a conversation between his father and the man who was to be his tutor and quoted Macrobius in the original.

His first instructor was a Dame Oliver and so apt a pupil was he that he could read Shakespeare almost as a child. Before he was to leave for Oxford, this worthy woman brought him "a present of gingerbread, and said he was the best scholar she ever had," a compliment which pleased Johnson mightily even in recollection. At the age of ten he began to learn Latin with an under-master of Lichfield School. He had another year at the Grammar School at Stourbridge and passed the subsequent two years at home, being "scolded by his father for his want of steady application . . . Yet he read a great deal in a desultory manner." He worked in his father's shop and, according to Hawkins, even learned to bind books; as late as 1819 it was said in Lichfield that books which Johnson had bound were still in existence. The boy Samuel must have given rather sorry promise from a worldly point of view, for his uncle, Cornelius Ford, said to him; "You will make your way the more easily in the world, I see, as you are content to dispute no man's claims to conversation excellence, and they will, therefore, more willingly allow your pretensions as a writer." This Ford was a profligate clergyman from whom Hogarth is supposed to have drawn the parson in his riotous Modern Midnight Conversation.

When he was nineteen Johnson's name was entered on the books of Pembroke College, Oxford, but he held the instruction of his tutor, Mr. Jorden, in such low esteem that he attended him irregularly. Poverty made him audacious rather than servile, and the promise of his dominance in talk was given then, for, tattered as he was, he would often harangue the younger men of the college under the gate of Pembroke and hold them spellbound with his wit and learning, for which at least one classmate remembered him forty-nine years later when they met accidentally on a London street. "We all feared him," said Oliver Edwards. But poverty compelled him to quit in 1731, although the researches of Aleyn Lyell Reade have led him to the conclusion that Johnson's Oxford residence terminated in 1729. "The friend to whom he had trusted for support had deceived him." The generosity to which he was indebted for his Oxford residence was not sufficiently long-winded. He may have had in mind the small sums for which he was indebted to Oxford tradesmen—although he had future occasions for learning the same lesson—when he wrote this bit of wisdom in a letter in 1759 to Joseph Simpson, a school-fellow who became a barrister, but "fell into a dissipated course of life": "Small debts are like small shot; they are rattling on every side, and can scarcely be escaped without a wound." He returned to Lichfield in worse case than he had left it. He found his father insolvent, himself at a loss what to do. His father died in December of 1731 and in the middle of the following July he wrote in his diary: "I layed by eleven guineas on this day, when I received twenty pounds, being all that I have reason to hope for out of my father's effects."

Five years were to elapse before he was to storm the citadel of London. During this period he was employed as usher in the school of Market-Bosworth, in Leicestershire, in which employment he suffered what Boswell described as "intolerable harshness;" dwelt for a time in Birmingham, within which period he translated Lobo, and married in 1736 a widow twice his age, Mrs. Elizabeth Porter, who had a daughter, Lucy, only six years younger than her foster-father and an inheritance of several hundred pounds which went into the purchase and upkeep of the ill-fated school at Edial. Johnson called it a love-match on both sides, thought her beautiful, regarded her praise of his Rambler essays more pleasing than that of anybody else and treasured her memory in his Prayers and Meditations long after she had passed away, in 1752. He always thought and wrote of her affectionately, and 26 years after her death, in speaking of her to his old college-mate, Edwards, he could say, "in a solemn, tender, faultering tone": "I have known what it was to *lose a wife* —It had almost broke my heart."

Garrick, one of the pupils of the school which the Johnsons conducted at Edial, near Lichfield, has left, through Boswell, a rather pathetic-humorous account of the affection displayed by the Johnsons for each other, as perceived by "the young rogues" through the key-hole of the Johnsons' bed-chamber, "that they might turn into ridicule his tumultuous and awkward fondness for Mrs. Johnson, whom he used to name by the familiar appellation of *Tetty*, or *Tetsey*, which like *Betty* or *Betsey*, is provincially used as a contraction for *Elizabeth*, her christian name, but which to us seems ludicrous, when applied to a woman of her age and appearance." However precious she may have been to Johnson—and there is evidence enough that the lonely Johnson regarded her as his only friend and companion—this is what she was to an emotionally uninvolved observer, Garrick: "very fat, with a bosom of more than ordinary protuberance, with swelled cheeks of a florid red, produced by thick painting, and increased by the liberal use of cordials; flaring and fantastick in her dress, and affected both in her speech and general behaviour." And Boswell adds: "I have seen Garrick exhibit her, by his exquisite talent of mimickry, so to excite the heartiest bursts of laughter." Poor Johnson! Not even in the brief period of an awkward love was he to be vouchsafed any privacy. But the images of herself which Mrs. Johnson threw on the mirrors of other minds than Garrick's were flattering. At no time did Johnson respect empty-headed prettiness. He liked intelligent, though not "learned" women.

The academy at Edial closed in a year and a half and Johnson left to try his fortune in London, accompanied by his bright pupil, Garrick, who, destined for the law, was to complete his education at an academy kept by one Mr. Colson. Johnson had a couple of guineas and three acts of his tragedy "Irene" which Garrick, twelve years later when he was at the height of his power, was to produce at Drury Lane. But meanwhile, though little is known of Johnson's early London years, certainly not until the year which is supposed to mark the turn of the tide, 1747, it is safe to assume that he shared—although not to the same degree—the lot of such typical Grub Street poets as Samuel Boyse and Richard Savage. Boyse would write Latin verses in bed when his shirts had been pledged, with his arms through holes in the blanket and appear in public with strips of white paper serving for cuffs and neckband and minus his breeches; he died in utter destitution. Savage, the son of an earl, and a shoemaker's apprentice by trade, homicide, blackmailer, and impostor, would sleep in the winter months as close as he could get to the furnace of a glass house and died in Bristol Prison in 1743. But he had charm and graciousness and he was a poet. George Psalmanazar, a Frenchman who posed as a Japanese convert to Christianity and who, after undeceiving the English public, finished his days in sanctity, dying in 1763, was mentioned to Boswell as the one whom Johnson sought after "the most." "I used to go and sit with him at an alehouse in the city."

It was the memory of those days that made

Johnson later fear for his salvation, for male poets did not constitute his only company at the taverns. "His amorous inclinations were uncommonly strong and impetuous . . . He used to take women of the town to taverns, and hear them relate their history." Which, by itself, proves rather humane curiosity than amorous impetuosity. Since Boswell did not give us particulars of Johnson's amorous life shall we conclude that it was because there was something to hide or because there was nothing? The puritanical Hawkins is less discreet, and only more confusing, but he makes it apparent that Johnson had some un-metaphysical causes for disturbance. Savage is definitely presented as that evil genius who initiated Johnson into the vices of the town and was responsible for a temporary separation of the Johnsons, elsewhere explained on the ground of Mrs. Johnson's ill-health. Yet it seems as if a negative remorse, as much as a positive love, dictated the memorial references to his Tetty which Johnson sprinkled through his Prayers and Meditations and at times through his conversation years after her death. Hawkins

JOHNSON'S GOUGH SQUARE HOME

No. 17 Gough Square, where Johnson wrote the Dictonary. This house is now a Johnson memorial. From a drawing by A. L. Collins

tells us that although he has no substantial justification for asserting that Johnson was infected with the vices of the town, yet, " I have reason to think, that he reflected with as little approbation on the hours he spent with Savage as on any period of his life." Hawkins also tells us that after the adjournment of the Ivy Lane Club, so unwilling was Johnson to go to his lodgings, that he would walk the streets and talk with the " miserable females " he met, asking them about their course of life, the history of their seduction and their chances of reclamation. But the most provokingly incomplete statement in Hawkins " Life " is that Johnson " talked of secret transgressions, and seemed desirous of telling me more than I was willing to hear." And Mrs. Thrale tells us how Johnson after having walked with her son as far as the garden gate, praying audibly for his salvation, said to her suddenly, " Make your boy tell you his dreams; the first corruption that entered into my heart was communicated in a dream." She asked him about it. " ' Do not ask me.' " replied he with violence, and walked away in apparent agitation."

We are told by Johnson of one woman of the town he knew, Bet Flint, whom he called a wit.

"'Bet Flint!' cried Mrs. Thrale, 'pray who is she?'"

"'Oh, a fine character, Madam! She was habitually a slut and a drunkard, and occasionally a thief and a harlot.'"

It seems that she had written some verses which she had brought to Johnson to correct and that he gave her, instead of correction, half a crown. She was arrested for the theft of a quilt and, when acquitted, decided to make a petticoat out of it. Once at dinner at Mr. Dilly's he again referred to her in almost the same words.

One of the earliest Johnson anecdotes which Boswell heard at Hume's house in Edinburgh some time before he came to London, referred to Johnson's visiting behind the scenes of Drury Lane. He said he had been well entertained, Mr. Garrick therefore hoped to see him often. Boswell felt compelled to state his reply in euphemistic paraphrase: "I'll come no more behind your scenes, David: for the silk stockings and the white bosoms of your actresses excite my amorous propensities." However little we may know about Johnson's amorous life, we may surmise that it was for sins more mortal than pouring milk into tea on Good Friday that he was frightened, although he was generally over-severe, morally, with himself. He trembled for his salvation, and he continued trembling for his salvation almost up to the last. He feared that he had not fulfilled the conditions on which salvation is granted and that he would be damned. And when Dr. Adams, the master of Pembroke College, asked the gloomy moralist what he meant by "damned," he replied, passionately and loudly, "Sent to Hell, Sir, and punished everlastingly." His Hell was no literary device and his sin was not purely of the imagination, although its weight bore him down long after he might have been expected to have marked his conquest of it. Yet he must have exaggerated. When Sir John Hawkins read for the dying Johnson a letter from the Rev. Mr. Winstanley who wrote that "on the near approach of death, what you once considered mere peccadilos have risen into mountains of guilt, while your best actions have dwindled into nothing," the Doctor interrupted: "*Does he say so?* Read it again! Sir John." Whatever the real occasion for fear, he was to some extent what he charged Boswell with being, a moth over the flame, his own tormentor.

The days of his association with Savage and Psalmanazar were the days of starvation alternated with gluttony and of nights when he tramped the streets for lack of shelter, or found dubious rest in the corner of some cellar. Years later he revealed that it was customary for him to go without food two days at a time, having tea without bread and paying his visits only at non-dining hours and, whenever possible, on the clean shirt day of the week. During those years he learned to fast from Sunday's dinner to Tuesday's dinner. The fierceness with which he was accustomed to attack his food—"the veins of his forehead swelled, and generally a strong perspiration was visible"—testified to the nature of habits learned in poverty. He knew abstinence, but not temperance, as he himself had testified. "And have you not observed," he asked Mrs. Thrale in a letter, "that my *genius* is always in extremes; that I am very noisy, or very silent; very gloomy, or very merry; very sour, or very kind? And would you have me cross my *genius* when it bids me sometimes to voracity and sometimes to abstinence?"

Johnson's first London lodgings were in the house of a stay-maker, in Exeter Street, adjourning Catherine Street, in the Strand. "I dined very well for eight-pence, with very good company, at the Pine Apple, in New Street, just by . . . It used to cost the rest of a shilling, for they drank wine; but I had a cut of meat for six-pence, and bread for a penny, and gave the waiter a penny; so that I was quite well served, nay, better than the rest, for they gave the waiter nothing." During his early drinking days he occasionally visited a tavern on Catherine Street, where he had half a pint of wine and if he were hungry and had the price, a mutton pie to boot. Sometimes he was fed at the house of Harry Hervey and he used to say to

Boswell, "if you call a dog Hervey, I shall love him." Unlike many of his colleagues, violent and irascible as he could be, he knew gratitude and those early days in London strengthened the seed of pity which always had been implanted in him. His treatment of that technically criminal and in many ways antipodal character Savage, with whom he roamed the streets at night for lack of shelter, is among the most eloquent examples in Johnson's life of wide humanity superseding narrow principle.

It was about a year after his first arrival in London that he obtained a finger-hold as a writer, through Edward Cave, who, under the name of Sylvanus Urban, carried on The Gentleman's Magazine, founded in 1731. It was at Cave's establishment, at St. John's Gate, Clerkenwell, that Johnson first met Savage, who was, in his time, esteemed a considerable poet. In fact, he regarded himself as a serious candidate for the laureateship before it was conferred on Colley Cibber. The Gentleman's Magazine was for many years the principal, and almost sole, repository of Johnson's drudge-work as well as of some examples of his typical genius, such as The Life of Richard Savage, of which he wrote forty-eight of the printed octavo pages at a sitting, working all night. This, although published anonymously early in 1744, helped strengthen Johnson's growing reputation, although even after it was published he was obliged to dine behind a screen in Mr. Cave's lodgings lest his wretched apparel be seen by Mr. Cave's guest, Mr. Harte. Johnson had already published, in 1738 a poem, "London," based on one of Juvenal's satires, a poem which had earned the approbation of Pope himself, with whose work it was favorably compared. In fact, Johnson's poem outsold a satire of Pope's which was published the same day. Pope was then the only man living in England who had become rich by his pen alone. He tried to obtain a degree and the mastership of a grammar school for the author of "London," but failed.

Johnson was fated to scribble on, one of his jobs consisting in reporting Parliamentary debates, largely through his imagination, on the basis of the most meagre notes, and sometimes none. He always gave the Tory side his best arguments and his best prose, seeing to it that "the Whig dogs should not have the best of it." Two of the speeches Johnson wrote later appeared in Lord Chesterfield's miscellaneous works, one being compared to Demosthenes, the other to Cicero, and he invented a speech for Chatham which is still believed to be Chatham's own. Johnson put bad arguments into Robert Walpole's mouth but his son Horace denied that his animosity to Johnson originated in the Parliamentary Debates he wrote for this periodical. Toward the latter part of his life Johnson said that these debates were the only part of his writings which gave him any compunction and he is said to have discontinued writing them when he learned that one had been translated as authentic into German, French and Spanish. He wrote also poems, essays, biographies, translations. Then, and later, Johnson wrote so much that not even his prodigious memory was capable of the task of recalling all the items of his bibliography. Although he disliked to write dedications for his own works, he wrote many for others, including one for Percy's "Reliques" and for Reynolds's first seven "Discourses"; and during the whole stretch of his writing career, forty sermons which he sold or gave away to clergymen who were less fertile in pious themes. Dr. Taylor was Johnson's chief beneficiary in that respect. About 1756, a living in Lincolnshire, in the gift of Langton's father, was offered to him, but he refused, acknowledging that his temper and habits rendered him unfit, and, besides, so deeply did he love London that he would feel like an exile out of it.

Johnson's contributions to The Gentleman's Magazine slacked in 1743 and stopped the following year. He did some cataloguing, of the Library of the Earl of Oxford, wrote a preface for the first volume of the catalogue, being employed in that task by a bookseller by the name of Osborne who is remembered because Johnson distinguished him by knocking him down with a folio. "Sir," he said to Boswell, "he was impertinent to me and I beat him." Dr. Hill, in a footnote, gives us the title of the very learned and equally obscure book with which the deed was done. The years 1745 and 1746 seem to be shrouded in darkness, and it is believed that Johnson's disappearance from the scene at that time had something to do with the Jacobite Rebellion, but that is purely legendary. However, for the four-year period, 1745–48, not a single letter from him is extant. In 1747, the year which is supposed to mark the turn of his fortunes, he undertook to write, for a committee of London booksellers, a Dictionary of the English Language, in two folio volumes, promising to complete it in three years, for the stipulated sum of 1575 pounds. Johnson then drew up the Plan and, at Robert Dodsley's suggestion addressed it to Lord Chesterfield, to whom the Dictionary might have been dedicated had not the touchy lexicographer been given some cause for offense. Whatever it was, the flattering letters Chesterfield published in The World just before the Dictionary came out, in 1755, failed to soothe Johnson either into a pardon or a dedication. That affair produced, however, that manly letter in which the most independent author of his age wrote his death-dealing definitions of patron and patronage. The task of producing the Dictionary was a longer and more arduous one than the sanguine Johnson had anticipated. Dr. Adams, calling on Johnson one day, at his Gough Square home, where the greater part of the Dictionary was written, and where it was finished, found him busy at work. "But, Sir," he asked, "how can you do this in three years?" "JOHNSON. Sir, I have no doubt that I can do it in three years. ADAMS. But the French Academy, which consists of forty members, took forty years to compile their Dictionary. JOHNSON. Sir, thus it is. This is the proportion. Let me see; forty times forty is sixteen hundred. As three to sixteen hundred, so is the proportion of an Englishman to a Frenchman." However, the task took him eight years, with the help of six amanuenses, thus reducing, somewhat, the disparity between a Frenchman and an Englishman.

But not so much, for within the period devoted to Dictionary-making, he produced what is regarded as his greatest poem, "The Vanity of Human Wishes," (1749), the first work to bear his name; revived the periodical essay, one of the century's characteristic productions, with the series known under the collective title of "The Rambler," begun March 20, 1750, and ended March 14, 1752; contributed a series of essays to The Adventurer, which John Hawkesworth, an imitative Johnsonian, edited from Nov. 7, 1752, to March 9, 1754, and he contributed also various pieces for The Gentleman's Magazine, not to mention other literary odds and ends, such as dedications and probably sermons. It was during this period that Garrick produced Johnson's "Irene" at Drury Lane, the author appearing on the first night in all his glory, in a scarlet waistcoat, with rich gold lace and a gold-laced hat. It was about this time that he organized The Ivy Lane Club, which met at the King's Head, a famous beef-steak house on that thoroughfare, all the surviving members of which, including Hawkins, were regarded as possessing a prescriptive right to join The Club, when that was formed about a dozen years later.

Johnson suffered his most distracting sorrow

in the midst of his Dictionary labors. The death of his beloved Tetty in 1752 removed that one dear friend to whom he referred when he wrote Chesterfield that the notice taken of his labors had been delayed, "till I am solitary and cannot impart it." That night on which she died Johnson was "all but wild with excess of sorrow," until soothed by prayer with a friend. No Academy ever produced a Dictionary "amidst inconveniences and distraction, in sickness and in sorrow" such as Johnson suffered. And he was in need too, sometimes in such straits that he was compelled to threaten that he would strike work as a counter-move to the booksellers' threat to put a blockade on his weekly payments, probably because of the extensions of time Johnson had been requiring. (He received more than 100 pounds above the stipulated sum.) Long after their work for him was done, Johnson strove hard to alleviate the bitter lot of two of his most unfortunate amanuenses, Peyton and Alexander Macbean—there were two Macbeans among his amanuenses—digging into his own pockets and begging for them on every hand.[1] And twice within the year following the publication of the Dictionary Johnson himself was arrested for debt, on both occasions being freed by Richardson, an author who was wise enough to keep his printing shop that his shop might keep him.

Not even in the Dictionary could Johnson exclude his personal humors and prejudices. His Scottish prejudice is reflected in his definition of oats as "A grain which in England is generally given to horses, but in Scotland supports the people;" his Tory prejudice in the definition of a Whig as "The name of a faction." Grub street is "the name of a street in London, so much inhabited by writers of small histories, *dictionaries,* and temporary poems" and a lexicographer is a "writer of dictionaries; a harmless drudge." Even his moral prejudices found ex-

[1] Through Johnson's intercession this Macbean was admitted into the Charterhouse, where he died, in the year of Johnson's death. Peyton died a few days after his wife, all expiring under the most wretched circumstances. They were buried at Johnson's expense.

pression in omissions. When some young women complimented him on having omitted the naughty words, he replied: "So, my dears, you have been looking for them." His definition of network is quoted as an example of how a simple fact may be obscured by Latinity in definition: "Anything reticulated or decussated, at equal distances, with interstices between the intersections." In the preface, in which he referred to those "few wild blunders and risible absurdities" which might for a time "furnish folly with laughter, and harden ignorance in contempt," he asked this amazing question: "When the radical idea branches out into parallel ramifications, how can a constructive series be formed of senses in their nature collateral?" He describes a cough as "a convulsion of the lungs, vellicated by some sharp serosity." And an example of Johnson's revision of his own simple, vigorous speech into Latinism is his parallel judgment on the play, The Rehearsal. At first he said, "The Rehearsal has not wit enough to keep it sweet." Then considering; "It has not vitality enough to preserve it from putrefaction." It was in talk, and not in writing, that he gave that vigorous definition of patriotism, perhaps his best remembered definition, as "the last refuge of a scoundrel." It was said by the waggish that Johnson used long words to show how necessary was a large folio Dictionary.[2]

The inauguration of The Universal Chronicle, or Weekly Gazette, gave Johnson his next important opportunity. It was for this paper that he wrote his most famous series of periodical essays, "The Idler," which, begun April 15, 1758, appeared every Saturday until April 5, 1760, a brisker, lighter, less Latinish piece of

[2] It is rather by such "risible absurdities" of his as his relaxed vigilance overlooked that we think we know Johnson in his characteristic expression. It is so much more tempting to identify a man by his caricature than by his portrait. Johnson, however, was only intermittently Johnsonese. Take him at his best, in "The Vanity of Human Wishes," some of his essays, some of "The Lives of the Poets," and the preface to his Shakespeare Edition, many of his definitions and some of his letters and you will find words which, even if they are not winged, are simple and vigorous in thought and when their maker wishes them to be, appealing to the emotions.

work which was written, as Arthur Murphy observed, "with abated vigour, in a style of ease and unlaboured elegance." In this series appears his most famous character, Dick Minim, the critic, Mr. Sober representing none other than the author, and Jack Whirler being an affectionate caricature of John Newbery, that busy patent medicine agent and bookseller. Langton and Reynolds contributed a few of the essays. During this period Johnson was engaged also in getting together his materials for the promised edition of Shakespeare, for which he had published Proposals in 1756. The death of his mother, in January 1759 created the need for funds with which to pay her funeral expenses and discharge her final debts.

In harmony with the spirit of the occasion which called it forth, he wrote a novelized essay on the choice of life, a prose statement of the philosophy of "The Vanity of Human Wishes," namely "Prince of Abissinia." This, strangely enough, was not published under the title by which it is generally known, "Rasselas," until after the author's death. Johnson wrote it in the evenings of a week, sending the sheets to the printer without looking at them. Not only did it serve the purpose for which it was written, earning 100 pounds, and a subsequent bonus of 25, but it also diffused the name of Johnson more than any other previous work of his, outselling even "The Vicar of Wakefield" and being translated abroad into almost every foreign language, although most of the translations did not appear until after the author's death. Nevertheless, it was as awkward a novel as "Irene" was as a drama, the Abyssinians talking in Johnsonian periods and expressing Johnsonian sentiments. Imlac, the philosopher in the novel, was the name which Boswell, in a letter to Mrs. Thrale, playfully applied to Johnson. "Rasselas" illustrates the general inflexibility of Johnson's serious and moralizing style, a point which Goldsmith made with some humor against Johnson himself. Reynolds, Goldsmith and Johnson were together one day when Goldsmith said he thought he could write a fable and observed that few writers could succeed in making animals talk in character, referring to the

Dear Madam

If I write but seldom to you, it is because it seldom happens that I have any thing to tell you that can give you pleasure, but last Monday I was sent for by the chief Minister the Earl of Bute, who told me that the King had empowered him to do something for me, and let me know that a pension was granted me of three hundred a year. Be so kind as to tell Kitty. I am

Dearest Madam

July 24. 1762 Your most affectionate

Sam: Johnson

To Miss Porter

in Lichfield

DR. JOHNSON SENDS NEWS

Facsimile letter, written to Lucy Porter, his step-daughter, informing her he has obtained a pension

fable of the little fishes who saw birds flying over them and petitioned Jupiter to change them into birds. "The skill (continued he), consists in making them talk like little fishes. While he indulged himself in this fanciful reverie, he observed Johnson shaking his sides and laughing. Upon which he smartly proceeded, 'Why Dr. Johnson, that is not so easy as you seem to think; for if you were to make little fishes talk, they would talk like WHALES.'"

In 1762, the Tories having, at last, returned to power, Lord Bute offered Johnson an annual pension of 300 pounds, what though he had defined pension in his Dictionary as "pay given to a state hireling for treason to his country," and pensioner as a slave of trade hired to obey his master. He debated with himself whether to take it, but finally accepted. The 300 pounds put a quietus to Johnson's Jacobitism. He decided that it hardly would be honest to drink James's health with George's liquor. "I think," he said, "the pleasure of cursing the House of Hanover and drinking King James's health all amply overbalanced by three hundred pounds a year." In the words of Lord Bute, the pension, which freed him for the rest of his life and freed him, moreover, for his matchless talk, "is not given you for anything you are to do, but for what you have done." Nevertheless, it was upon some political prompting that he wrote such pamphlets as The False Alarm and Taxation no Tyranny which even in his own time and among his own friends did nothing to enhance his reputation. The year after the pension was granted Boswell began paying court and it is of the greatest moment that Boswell entered the scene just about the time when Johnson was most free to indulge his greatest talent. This sequence of events was so fortunate and so delightful in its consequences that it seems to have been of the kind which Fate arranges for us only when she is in the most beneficent of moods. No two events of Johnson's life are comparable in importance and in pleasurable consequences for us than the granting of the pension and the crossing of Johnson's and Boswell's trails.

After 1763 the chief events in Johnson's life, except for the happy connection with the

Thrale family, consisted in the things he said, the judgements he delivered, the conversations he dominated, and the clean thoroughness with which he despatched antagonists. The organization of The Club is less important than the meeting of Johnson and Boswell and Johnson's association with the Thrales, but remains, nevertheless, among the most important post-pension episodes. The Club, sometimes referred to as The Literary Club, was founded in 1764, Johnson and Reynolds being the prime movers. It met originally at the Turk's Head Tavern, which stood at Greek and Compton Streets, Soho, before it was removed to Gerard Street, not far away. They met at first for weekly suppers and then fortnightly. The combined puff of its members was sufficient to sell out a recommended book, while a reverse decision could kill. Fanny Burney's first novel, "Evelina," for example had the combined suffrage of Burke, Gibbon, Reynolds, and Johnson. Other members of the club included Goldsmith, Garrick, Percy, Boswell, Fox, and Sheridan. In 1765 there was published after a long delay which had tried the patience of anxious subscribers who had long ago put their money down, an eight-volume edition of the plays of Shakespeare, edited and prefaced by Johnson, the vitality of which work can be gauged by the controversy it incited; few, however, are inclined to disagree with Adam Smith in his praise of the clear and vigorous Preface. In the same year Trinity College, Dublin, created him Doctor of Laws.

From that year too dates the almost life-long friendship with the Thrales of Southwark and Streatham, Henry Thrale being a rich brewer, a good liver and an intelligent man of that sturdy quality which Johnson could admire. He sat in Parliament from December 1765 until the dissolution of 1780. Boswell referred to him as one who loved to have the wits about his house, but was not a wit himself. Mrs. Thrale, a young woman of intelligence and vivacity, pretty and clever, ministered to Johnson when he was ill and bore the moralist's reproofs and exactions with the best of temper, in her husband's lifetime, anyway. But she was repaid with the distinction which his company shed upon her home and with the occasion for the writing of an entertaining book about him. For sixteen years he enjoyed their hospitality, at Streatham in the summer and at Southwark in the winter, making it a habit to be at his own lodgings in gloomy Bolt Court at week-ends in order that he might give Sunday dinners to such poor friends and dependents as might otherwise have gone without. During his regular absences from his lodgings, which he took in 1776 and in which he died, his ill-assorted houseful of dependents would wage war among themselves and even Johnson would sometimes submit to being driven forth by their quarrels rather than exert his authority. Hawkins also expressed his amazement at the manner in which Johnson bowed his head to the insults of Levett and the bad temper of Mrs. Williams. Lapses which he would not suffer from the powerful he readily forgave in the wretched, as much from principle as from his profound instinct of pity. He would sometimes allow himself to be driven from his own house, and Mrs. Thrale has testified: "He really was oftentimes afraid of going home, because he was so sure to be met at the door with numberless complaints; and he used to lament pathetically to me . . . that they made his life miserable from the impossibility he found of making theirs happy, when every favor he bestowed on one was wormwood to the rest." As he wrote to her: "Williams hates everybody; Levet hates Desmoulines, and does not love Williams, Desmoulines hates them both. Poll [Miss Carmichael] loves none of them." And on another occasion: "Discord keeps her residence in this habitation, but she has for some time been silent. We have much malice, but no mischief." The Thrales provided Johnson with the happiest refuge of his life, enabling him not only to live at peace, but to pass on to others a larger part of his pension than he might otherwise have been able to give away.

Johnson first met the Thrales at the beginning of 1765 at their home at Southwark, near the Thrale brewery. Together with Woodhouse, a poetical shoemaker, Johnson was brought to them by Murphy. He thereafter became a regular guest at the Thrales's Thursday dinner parties. It was in the following year, 1766, that Johnson made one of the Thrale household. The circumstance which occasioned the "adoption" of Johnson was characteristic enough. The Thrales calling one morning on the great man heard him "in the most pathetic terms," implore the prayers of a clergyman who had just left. It appears that Johnson was praying to be saved from insanity. Mrs. Thrale was affected with grief at the spectacle, but her husband was so shocked that, involuntarily, he lifted his hand to close Johnson's mouth against his confessions and fears. The Thrales carried him off to their Streatham home in Streatham Park, Surrey, six miles from Westminster Bridge, and at both of the Thrale residences he was assigned a room, and became a member of the household and a loving elder to the Thrale children. In 1769, seventeen years after the death of his Tetty, one of the Thrale babies was christened Lucy Elizabeth, in memory of that long-dead wife and the adopted widower was named the child's god-father. He might have died in one of those rooms, instead of in his own less brightly furnished lodgings, had not Mrs. Thrale, after her husband's death in 1781, from over-indulgence at table, (to which vice he abandoned himself the more thoroughly upon the death of his son) shown a disinclination to board and lodge Johnson. As much as she pretended to feel "veneration for his virtue, reverence for his talents, delight in his conversation," and however much he helped make her reputation as a hostess and gave her her greatest opportunities for authorship, she nevertheless asserted that he domineered over her household, commanded her servants, her carriage and her time, and never spoke to her but to blame and deride. The company of the great and the admired Dr. Johnson is suddenly represented in her "Anecdotes" as "a yoke my husband first put upon me." Her infatuation for the singer, Gabriel Piozzi of Brescia, and her marriage to him made sure the lifting of that yoke. However, Johnson was not the man to forget that it had been her kindness which had "soothed twenty years of a life radically wretched."

The association, however terminated, was pure gain to both. Johnson made a rich brewer's house one of the salons of London, inferior only to Mrs. Vesey's. But much as Johnson may have conferred, he received far more. Under the Thrale roof life took on a more happy and tranquil pace. His life was probably prolonged because of the Thrales and to that prolonged period we owe his best work, the one which has been the most certain preservative of his reputation, the "Lives of the Poets." He relaxed and blossomed, became playful, indulged in more outdoor exercise, such as fox-hunting, submitted a little to the softening influence of family life and the company of women and learned, at times, to modulate the tiger's roar to a cat-like purr. Thrale could make him "suppress many rough answers" with which he might have hurt the feelings of others at the Thrale board. It was Thrale who persuaded him to put silver buckles on his shoes and to "change his shirt, his coat and his plate almost before it became indispensably necessary to the comfortable feeling of his friends." As a result of Thrale's influence, Johnson bought better clothes, enlivening the dark cloth with metal buttons, and he enjoyed even frequent changes of his wigs, the foreparts of which used to be singed by his too close application to the candle because of his short-sightedness. Only the masterful brewer dared turn off the spigot of Johnson's talk without suffering lashing reproof, if we are to believe Mrs. Thrale, who tells us that her husband once cut short the great Johnson with: "There, there, now, we have had enough for one lecture, Dr. Johnson; we will not be upon education any more till after dinner, if you please."

It was with the Thrales that Johnson enjoyed some of his longest travels, accompanying them to Wales and France, and he also went with them on various trips to Brighton. He would have accompanied them on their proposed journey to Italy, but for the death of their only son Harry, in 1776, which put an end to the plan for that year, and for all time. Yet, but for Mrs. Thrale's seconding of Boswell's plea, Johnson might not have undertaken, in 1773, that famous journey to the Hebrides. This trip resulted in Johnson's "A Journey to the Western Islands of Scotland," which when he read it in manuscript, made George III wonder whether Johnson was not yet somewhat of a Stuart adherent and a Papist into the bargin, the very reasons for which, Walpole implied, the King had been made to give him a pension—for conversion's sake, presumably. Two years later Oxford granted him the honorary degree of Doctor of Laws. In 1779 were published the first four volumes, and, in 1781, the last six, of "Lives of the Poets," a work undertaken at the request of a committee of London booksellers who wished brief biographical prefaces to the works of poets —of their own selection—to be issued in a new edition. On May 3, 1777, a little less than a month after the booksellers' committee had called, he wrote to Boswell: "I am engaged to write little Lives, and little Prefaces, to a little edition of *The English Poets.* I think I have persuaded the booksellers to insert something of Thomson." By his recommendation were added also Blackmore, Watts, Pomfret and Yalden.

Johnson gave the booksellers, instead of the prefaces, solid chapters of biography, rich in anecdote in cases of contemporary or almost-contemporary poets, and rich also in criticism expressive of his intense prejudices, particularly against Gray, Milton and Prior, among others.

Three more years of life were vouchsafed Johnson. Thrale having died in 1781, the brewer's Streatham home, the setting of Johnson's happiest and most comfortable years, was let, the following year. The relation between Johnson and Mrs. Thrale continued superficially in the course in which it had so smoothly run in the life of the master, but only Johnson seemed unaware, up to the last, of the love which had taken possession of Mrs. Thrale's bosom. In 1783, Johnson founded the Essex Head Club, after the name of the tavern at No. 40 Essex Street, Strand, in which sessions were held, to supply the want of company occasioned in part by the deaths of Mrs. Williams and Levett, as well as of Thrale. Reynolds, strangely enough, refused to join largely because of his disinclination to meet Barry with whom there had been words on the subject of the Academy and the Discourses. Two years before he had a club formed at the Queen's Arms, and in the last year, the survivors of the old Ivy Lane Club, organized many years before, were dined by Johnson. Even for part of 1783, he continued to make one of the Thrale household, although the bond was being definitely strained by Mrs. Thrale's impatience with Johnson's infirmities and hectorings. Towards the last his behavior became trying, for he would complain not only of the food, but of the guests of his hostess, while she found his table manners still far from polished. On one occasion when they had all gone off to Brighton, Mrs. Thrale, to escape him, ran off to Bath with her daughters. Dr. Hill calls her a deserter from Johnson, although, in all justice, it is probable that the deserted gave the deserter some cause.

The following year, 1784, his last, efforts were made to obtain for him either an increase in his pension, or an additional sum, from the government to enable him to spend that winter in Italy, where he would be able to breathe with less difficulty. Either the habits of poverty or the too human desire not to leave an insufficient sum to take care of the bequests he desired to make made him unwilling to touch his own hoard of 2000 pounds and he seemed to want to keep even the fact of its existence a secret. When, toward the last of June, the very day before their last meeting at Reynolds's, Boswell told him of the efforts being exerted to assure him the desired winter in Italy: "He listened with much attention; then warmly said, 'This is taking prodigious pains about a man.' 'O! Sir, (said I, with most sincere affection,) your friends would do everything for you.' He paused, grew more and more agitated, till tears started into his eyes, and he exclaimed with fervent emotion, 'God bless you all.' I was so affected that I also shed tears. After a short silence, he renewed and extended his grateful benediction, 'God bless you all, for Jesus Christ's sake.' We both remained for some time unable to speak. He rose suddenly and quitted the room, quite melted in tenderness."

A compromise offer, involving a mortgage on

WHERE JOHNSON DIED

No. 8 Bolt Court, where Samuel Johnson passed away, Dec. 13, 1784. This house is no longer standing.

his pension, was offered but Johnson felt well enough to visit his native Lichfield and Ashbourne, the home of his friend Dr. Taylor, early that Fall and he thought he could survive one more English winter. During his last months he arranged for the setting up of stones to mark the graves of wife, parents and brother. He returned to London in November, became worse, but although he was attended by some of the best physicians of the time, the dropsy and asthma from which he was suffering got the better of him. He spurred the physicians to make their incisions deeper but to no avail. Pains and discomforts relented, giving him false hope throughout his last year. Although Boswell was absent, Fanny Burney and the pious young Langton were among those who attended faithfully upon him. Langton, indeed, took lodgings in the vicinity that he might be near the old man. The old lion prayed, even if inaudibly. Several days before he died he sent for Reynolds and begged him to grant these requests: to remit a debt of 30 pounds that the sum might be diverted to a poor family, to read the Bible and not to draw on Sunday. Sir Joshua promised, and managed to keep all but the last. Before the end came he burned all his papers, overlooking, however, an autobiographical fragment on his childhood, up to the age of eleven, which Barber saved from the flames. On the day of his death, Dec. 13, 1784, a Miss Morris, daughter of a friend, called and begged for the Doctor's blessing. It was to her that he spoke his last words, "God bless you, my dear!" He passed away about seven that evening and a week later was laid to rest in Westminster Abbey.

CHAPTER SEVEN

"In His Last Will and Testament . . ."

IN his last will and testament Johnson projected beyond his life the good he had done during it. With his little hoard he might have prolonged his own life, but he wished perhaps for that limited degree of life after death which is hoped for from the gratitude of those upon whom benefits have been conferred. He had long intended that his chief beneficiary should be Francis Barber, the faithful Negro servant who had been with him almost without a break since 1752, whom he had educated and for whose release from naval service he had put himself to some trouble. On his death-bed Johnson asked Dr. Brocklesby, one of the physicians attending him, what would be regarded as a proper annuity to a favorite servant and was informed that the circumstances of the master governed the sum, but that in the case of a nobleman fifty pounds was considered adequate. "Then, (said Johnson,) shall I be *nobilissimus,* for I mean to leave Frank seventy pounds a year, and I desire you to tell him so." He hesitated to make a will, but was finally persuaded to do so. Including the annuity of seventy pounds, the bequest to Frank was estimated at a little less than 1500 pounds. This legacy angered Hawkins to the point of splenetic detraction, not even Barber's white wife escaping. He refers to Johnson having taken in during his last years Barber's wife and two daughters as an act committed "in the excess of indiscriminate benevolence," a Johnsonian phrase but a most un-Johnsonian sentiment. Hawkins accuses Johnson of having neglected a white relative in favor of a black servant, but the relative turns out to be one Mr. Heely who had married a cousin of Johnson's; she had died without issue, and Heely had married again. The naming of Barber as residuary legatee was lucky for Boswell in that it enabled him to obtain many papers not otherwise accessible.

To the estate of the late William Innys, bookseller, Johnson left 200 pounds, in consideration of help given by Mr. Innys to Johnson's father when the latter was a bankrupt, a debt of no less than fifty-three years' standing, repaid though both debtor and creditor had passed away. To a female servant, Mrs. White, he left 100 pounds, and a similar sum was provided for the maintenance of "Elizabeth Herne, a lunatick," for whose care he was so solicitous that he wrote, anticipating the bequest, as far back as February of the year of his death. He had long ago interested himself in the case of this poor girl, whom Hawkins called Johnson's first cousin. He left a number of other money bequests. To some of his friends he left specified books, and to others, including his physicians, a book apiece of their own selection "to keep as a token of remembrance." Fortunately, there was no clash. To James Boswell he left nothing, not even, as might have been expected, the literary executorship and Boswell is magnanimous enough to explain the omission on the ground that at the time Johnson could hardly be expected to think of any but those who were about him. That was generous in Boswell but the omission is significant in that it helps to prove that Boswell's superb achievement had led us to exaggerate the constancy of the relations between these two men.

Johnson might be rough in manner and sometimes cruel-spoken; he was incapable of recognizing the finer claims of sensitivity, but he needed no argument to enable him to recognize those of poverty and distress. In making this distinction he was emphasizing the limitations and the extensions of his own personality and experience. He had learned the wisdom of the proverb that "sticks and stones may break my bones, but names will never hurt me." When Boswell intimated that the roughness and harshness of the Johnsonian manner might give pain to persons of weak nerves, Johnson answered, "I know no such weak-nerved people," he himself not being weak-nerved. Yet he was as quick to apply the salve to a sensibility he had injured as he had been to inflict the wound. For what he termed "foppish lamentations" he could have neither understanding nor pity. Gray's notion that he could write only during certain hours must have seemed, at the least, "a fantastick foppery" to a man who had been compelled to write at all hours for his daily bread. He didn't care for finicky people, those who couldn't abide breaks in their polite routine, nor whiners at "metaphysical distresses." Occupation was the cure he prescribed for those bowed down by grief. "The poor and the busy have no time for sentimental sorrow," he said. For the madly devoted Lady Tavistock, who was dying of grief for her dead husband, he prescribed a job in a chandler's shop and a child to tend. Of one who was mourning the loss of a friend, he said: "Make him prime minister and see how long his friend will be remembered." Johnson would have thought the more highly of Goldsmith if that far from stoical Irishman had kept to himself his sense of disappointment at the failure of his play, "The Good Natured Man," and Mrs. Thrale drew from him a deserved rebuke when she expressed her annoyance at the dust of the road and its damage to her complexion. The dust raised by the Thrale carriage, the failure of a play, the loss of a loved husband were not in his mind occasions for tragic emotion in a world that was, in his phrase, bursting with sin and sorrow.

But one of the charms of Johnson was that he was human enough to violate those Stoic principles he set down for the guidance of mere weaklings. Although he took the failure of his own play " like the monument " the death of his wife reduced him to an agony of grief; he could weep at the loss of some friends and be melted quite at the death of others and one day while reading his own " Vanity of Human Wishes," the images of the past which it evoked made him break down into a " passion of tears." And sometimes he could whine not to be left alone, as if he were a child afraid of the dark—which, on second thought, he was. But, on the whole, he never made much of an exhibition of his own pains. " I will be conquered; I will not capitulate," he said before his death. His letters bespeak his good-natured contempt for valetudinarians, such as the Rev. Dr.

Seward, father of the "Swan of Lichfield," and Charles Congreve, a self-pampered school-fellow,[1] as they are eloquent of his constant readiness to give, beg and borrow for the benefit of those truly distressed. Mrs. Williams, Mrs. Carmichael, Mrs. Herne, Peyton and Macbean and Lowe are only a handful out of a large crowd. He sought to achieve impossibilities because his was the kind of Heaven that was accessible not to neuter goodness, but to positive exertions up to the hilt of one's capacity. "His daily terror lest he had not done enough," observed Mrs. Thrale, "originated in piety, but ended in little less than disease."

Since his own humble gifts, had they been multiplied many times, would not have equalled the necessities of which he was aware, he was constantly reminding richer friends of the wants he could not alleviate. As he wrote to Reynolds of one of his "cases:" "The man importunes me, and the blow goes round." Goldsmith, and

[1] Mrs. Thrale tells us of how Johnson admonished a clergyman who was complaining of his health. "Do not be like the spider, man; and spin conversation thus incessantly out of thy own bowels."

others who had had experience of the inner Johnson, could know that "he has nothing of the bear but his skin," but it was by his skin that the bear was known. Mrs. Thrale put it in another way, saying that "all he did was gentle, if all he said was rough," and she adds that he was looked upon as an "excepted" being who could do no wrong. He gave a tithe of more than one-tenth and surrendered something of his own comfort and convenience as well. It was estimated that he spent on himself, no more than 80 of the Crown's 300 pounds a year. We recall how, as far back as 1733, when he was doing his first hack job, a translation, he could not be brought to complete it until urged to do so on the ground that if he did not, the printer and his family must suffer need. We recall in what a rush he wrote "Rasselas" that his mother's funeral expenses and last debts might be paid, but in addition, he for many years contributed from his slender purse for her support in Lichfield, in the early London years undergoing want to alleviate her's. When Boswell, during the first year of his discipleship, not yet having been impregnated in the Johnsonian aether, expressed surprise to Goldsmith that Johnson should harbor a man who had so bad a reputation as the quack Levett—who drank hard because his patients were so poor that they could not pay him in anything but liquor—Goldsmith explained: "He (Levett) is now become miserable, and that insures the protection of Johnson," as beautiful a tribute of character as could be devised. This Levett was an unfortunate skinny scarecrow of a man who had, at the age of sixty, married a prostitute under the impression that she was an heiress, had been deserted by her and had then heard of her as on trial at the Old Bailey for picking pockets. Johnson respected his opinions, as physician and as man, but Levett gave none other an opportunity of judging his value since the presence of strangers served to close his lips. At two o'clock one morning as he was returning home along Fleet Street, Johnson found a woman of the town in the street, all but dead. He carried her home on his back, kept her under his roof for thirteen weeks, by which time she had recovered from some foul disease, raised some money for her and set her up as a milliner.

When a minister stopped Davies on the street to ask after Johnson, the former bookseller burst into tears, saying: "God for ever bless him. I am beholden to that good man for the bread I eat and the bed I lie on." Dr. Maxwell wrote: "He frequently gave all the silver in his pocket to the poor, who watched him, between his house and the tavern where he dined. He walked the streets at all hours and said he was never robbed, for the rogues knew he had little money, nor had the appearance of having much." His benevolence to Mrs. Williams was as long-lived as his patience with her temper was angelic. She had come to London to be cured of a cataract in both her eyes, was a regular visitor in the life-time of Mrs. Johnson, afterwards coming under the Johnson roof to conduct his household as well as her blindness would permit. And one day, on March 20, 1778, Boswell found Johnson at home with Mrs. Williams and was told "that the room formerly allotted to me was now appropriated to a charitable purpose; Mrs. Desmoulins, and I think her daughter, and a Miss Carmichael, all being lodged in it. Such was his humanity, and such his generosity, that Mrs. Desmoulins herself told me, he allowed her half-a-guinea a week. Let it be remembered, that this was above a twelfth part of his pension."

Hawkins couldn't interpret such humanity as anything but feeble-mindedness. What Hawkins tells us about Johnson illuminates both men. "He had a natural imbecility about him, arising from humanity and pity to the sufferings of his fellow-creatures, that was prejudicial to his interests." "As to Sir John," said Johnson, in a mock attempt to intercede for him amidst a hostile group, "why I really believe him to be an honest man at the bottom; but to be sure he is penurious and he is mean, and it must be owned he has a degree of brutality and a tendency to savageness that cannot easily be defended." Johnson's goodness extended to animals, certainly embracing the cat Hodge, from whose antics Boswell suffered some unease. Johnson himself would go out to buy oysters for Hodge, "lest the servants having that trouble should take a dislike to the poor creature." And he told Mrs. Thrale how he had once chided his wife for beating a cat before the maid, lest she do likewise, pleading the example of her mistress. Boswell contributes this most charming vignette of Johnson and Hodge: "I recollect him one day scrambling up Dr. Johnson's breast, apparently with much satisfaction, while my friend, smiling and half-whistling, rubbed down his back, and pulled him by the tail; and when I observed he was a fine cat, saying, 'Why yes, Sir, but I have had cats whom I liked better than this;' and then as if perceiving Hodge to be out of countenance, adding, 'but he is a very fine cat, a very fine cat indeed.'"

The quiet domesticity of this picture derives a more charming accent from the contrary scenes of gladiatorial combat in tavern and drawing room, combats of the kind we associate with the name of the great Cham. He called a tavern chair "the throne of human felicity," and whatever the chair in whch he sat, that was the throne. When Chesterfield, hoping that the

Dictionary might be dedicated to him, wrote several anonymous puffs for Johnson in The World, he suggested that Johnson be made the Dictator of the English language and be vested with the mantle of infallibility concerning all grammarian questions. But although Samuel Johnson never became Dictator of the language, he did seem to try to establish himself as monarch of talk. " Sir," said Goldsmith to Boswell, " you are for making a monarchy of what should be a republick." And Hawkins has left us this expression of Johnson's delight in tavern life: " As soon as I enter the door of a tavern I experience an oblivion of care, and a freedom from solicitude: when I am seated, I find the master courteous, and the servants obsequious to my call: anxious to know and ready to supply my wants: . . . I dogmatize and am contradicted, and in this conflict of opinions and sentiment I find delight." In view of the fact that Johnson was so much the club-man, in the social, rather than in the society, meaning of the word, it may be interesting to read the rules of one of those clubs, The Essex Head: " Every member is at liberty to introduce a friend once a week but not oftener: . . . Every member present at the Club shall spend at least a sixpence; and every member who stays away shall forfeit threepence . . . There shall be no general reckoning, but every man shall adjust his own expenses . . . One penny shall be left by each member for the waiter."

Johnson's child-like delight in a conversational tourney was such that he would sometimes maintain the wrong side, for contention's sake, "so that," as Boswell notes on the last page of his stupendous work, "when there was an audience, his real opinion could seldom be gathered from his talk; though when he was in company with a single friend, he would discuss a subject with genuine fairness." Once observing Johnson pause during a discussion as to whether card-playing was good or evil, Garrick remarked: "Now, he is thinking which side he shall take." But on another occasion the laugh was on Garrick. The actor was delivering a panegyric on Dryden, certainly one of Johnson's favorite poets, when the Doctor turned upon him and

THE FAMOUS PROFILE

From a mezzotint by James Watson, made in 1770, after the drawing by Sir Joshua Reynolds

dared him quote "twenty lines in a series that would not disgrace the poet and his admirer." He quoted a passage he had once heard Johnson praise, but Johnson saw fit this time to find an error in almost every line. Johnson once spoke so effectively in a wrong cause that his antagonist later conveyed his gratitude to him for having been argued out of a "vulgar error," upon hearing which Johnson remarked: "Nay, do not let him be grateful, for he was right, and I was wrong;" showing that however tempted he might be to battle for argument's sake, his pride did not demand that the error he had defended out of caprice be indefinitely sustained. Johnson's innate integrity is proved by the fact that it is not difficult to distinguish what he said in earnest from what he said in caprice.

He pretended to despise actors, but he was governed in part by the actor's motives. He did indeed go through some training for his role. He practiced talking, and told Reynolds of one rule by which he sought to govern himself; to talk his best, "whether the person to whom he addressed himself was or was not capable of comprehending him." Discussing Rousseau's social theories, for which he expressed such intense loathing that Boswell was compelled to beg to differ, Johnson informs us that he began in boyhood to perfect his dialectic powers. "When I was a boy," he told the company, "I used always to choose the wrong side of a debate, because most ingenious things, that is to say, most new things, could be said upon it." Not long after he put in practice this love of perverse argument. He was accompanying Boswell to Harwich in the coach from London. A fat elderly woman and a young Dutchman were their fellow-passengers. "The gentlewoman" beginning a violent tirade against the Roman Catholics, Johnson, "to the utter astonishment of all the passengers but myself . . . defended the Inquisition, and maintained, that 'false doctrine should be checked on its first appearance; that the civil power should unite with the church in punishing those who dared to attack the established religion, and that such only were punished by the Inquisition.'" Boswell knew that this was talk for the love of talk, but earlier in the day while they were dining at an inn, he had been somewhat disturbed by Johnson calling the attention of his fellow-passengers to himself and saying: "He was idle at Edinburgh. His father sent him to Glasgow, where he continued to be idle. He then came to London, where he has been very idle; and now he is going to Utrecht, where he will be as idle as ever." The delight in making even so slight a sally seemed to be worth the discomfiture of a new-made friend. He was never so pleased as when he had triumphed, as seemed to be the case most of the time. "Well, we had good talk," said Johnson to his Bozzy, returning one night from the Crown and Anchor, and Bozzy replied, with such obvious relish in his master's accomplishment, "Yes, Sir; you tossed and gored several persons."

But Boswell didn't like being gored himself and although he reports the fact that he was offended it is from another source that we learn the details. All he tells us is that "he attacked me with such rudeness, that I was vexed and angry, because it gave those persons [those present at Sir Joshua's on May 2, 1778] an opportunity of enlarging upon his supposed ferocity, and ill treatment of his best friends. I was so much hurt, and had my pride so much roused, that I kept away from him for a week; and, perhaps, might have kept away much longer, nay, gone to Scotland without seeing him again, had not we fortunately met and been reconciled. To such unhappy chances are human friendship liable." And six days after the snub, at Bennet Langton's, when Langton, having left them by themselves—" 'But why treat me so before people who neither love you nor me?' JOHNSON. 'Well, I am sorry for it. I'll make it up to you twenty different ways, as you please,' BOSWELL. 'I said today to Sir Joshua, when he observed that you *tossed* me sometimes—I don't care how often, or how high he tosses me, when only friends are present, for then I fall upon soft ground: but I do not like falling on stones, which is the case when enemies are present.—I think this is a pretty good image, Sir.' JOHNSON. 'Sir, it is one of the happiest I have ever heard.' " The painful thrust which came nearest to costing Johnson his Boswell was this. It was Boswell who gave Johnson the opening. "How delightful," he said, "it must have been to have lived in the society of Pope, Swift, Arbuthnot, Gay and Bolingbroke! We have no such society in our days." Sir Joshua observes an implied slur. "I think, Mr. Boswell, you might be satisfied with your great friend's conversation." "Nay, Sir," said Johnson, coming obviously to his young friend's rescue, "Mr. Boswell is right. Every man wishes for preferment, and if Boswell had lived in those days, he would have obtained promotion." "How so, Sir?" asked the host. "Why, Sir, he would have had a high place in the 'Dunciad.'" What a roar of laughter from the company, what pleasure reflected in Johnson's face at this sally, what confusion on Boswell's. He had indeed incited Johnson this time. But Boswell felt that as Johnson "had given me a thousand pounds in praise, he had a good right now and then to take a guinea from me." Another time when Johnson gave Boswell the rough side of his tongue, the pain was so intense that Boswell would not specify the insult and we have no other record of it, for it occurred at the Isle of Sky, during the Hebridean journey. Johnson had made a grave reference to keeping a seraglio, upon which Boswell had burst out laughing, whereupon Johnson " instantly retaliated with such keen sarcastick wit, and such a variety of degrading images of every one of which I was the object, that, though I can bear such attacks as well as most men, I yet found myself so much the sport of the company that I would gladly expunge from my mind every trace of this savage retort." About a fortnight before this outburst Boswell had greatly angered Johnson by riding ahead of him on the road—ostensibly to arrange for accomodations at the next inn—but Johnson would not accept an explanation and said that had Boswell gone on without attending to his shout, " I should have returned with you to Edinburgh, and then have parted from you, and never spoken to you more."

Johnson so patently talked for victory that he gave what he said a contentious accent, in such manner that Lord Pembroke could say to Boswell, with "some truth," as the latter admits, that "Dr. Johnson's sayings would not appear so extraordinary, were it not for his *bow wow* way." And Boswell makes a remark which makes us regret keenly the fact that the phonograph had not been invented in Johnson's day. Adjuring his readers to keep in mind, while reading his narrative, Johnson's "deliberate and strong utterance," he adds the regret that it cannot be preserved as music is written; declaring that the manner of his speech impregnated the matter and calling him, for the most part, a Handel of speech. He catches himself listening to Johnson's every sentence as to a musical composition. But it was strength rather than resononce that was generally recalled, Goldsmith applying to him a phrase out of one of Cibber's comedies: "There is no arguing with Johnson; for when his pistol misses fire, he knocks you down with the butt end of it," for he had evidently had a taste of Johnson's rough-house tactics, as when, having suggested that more members be added to The Club on the ground that "we have travelled over one another's minds," Johnson angrily retorted: "Sir, you have not travelled over *my* mind, I promise you." Reynolds, by nature a mild man, verifies this impression, for he says of Johnson: "He fought on every occasion as if his whole reputation depended upon the victory of the minute, and he fought with all the weapons. If he was foiled in argument, he had recourse to abuse and rudeness." His manner probably intimidated Gibbon and Charles James Fox, fellow-members of The Club, for the latter, despite his gifts, was always the listener and rarely the speaker, and the former would not cross swords with Johnson even when the subject was history, he having been heard to mutter, on one occasion, "I should not like to trust myself with *you*." Besides, both of these gentlemen were interested in ancient history and Johnson was not. Once when Fox tried to engage Johnson in conversation about Catiline's conspiracy, the Doctor withdrew his attention and thought about Tom Thumb. Gibbon's greatness seems to have been reserved largely for his books; there was none in his person; the ugly historian was as catty as he was vain. On Johnson's surprising allusion to Chesterfield's Letters: "Every man of any education would rather be called a rascal than be accused of deficiency in *the graces,"* a statement which, coming from none other than Johnson surprised the company somewhat, "Mr. Gibbon . . . turned to a lady who knew Johnson well, and lived much with him, and in his quaint manner, tapping his [snuff] box, addressed her thus: 'Don't you think, Madam (looking towards Johnson), that among all your acquaintances, you could find one exception?' " [2] No wonder Boswell called Gibbon "a venomous insect." Johnson, Boswell, and Walpole, at

[2] Johnson was sincere in the belief that he was a well-mannered man. "I look upon myself as a very polite man," he told Boswell, and once at the Thrales's, after he had done his best to put some Cambridge men in their place by boasting about Oxford, he declared, to the amazement of his hearers: "I am well-bred to a degree of needless scrupulosity. No man is so cautious not to interrupt another; no man thinks it so necessary to appear attentive when others are speaking; no man so steadily refuses preference to himself, or so willingly bestows it on another, as I do; no body holds so strongly as I do the necessity of ceremony, and the ill effects which follow the breach of it—yet people think me rude."

odds though they were on many things, were at one in their attitude toward the vain and ugly Gibbon. Johnson, no great beauty himself, had spoken with some disgust of Gibbon's ugliness; Walpole marvelled that the historian should avow his vanity " even about his ridiculous face and person " and Boswell, who normally loved eminence too much to hate men of eminence, wrote of him to Temple: " He is an ugly, affected, disgusting fellow and poisons our literary club for me." [3]

Johnson's manner, however rude it may have been, alienated not a single one of his friends, although it may have served to intimidate newcomers and to provoke short-lived lovers' quarrels. Not only Boswell, but Garrick, Reynolds, Langton and Goldsmith were occasional victims of his " humours." Their little differences may have intensified their affection. It was a characteristic of this great man that he defended be-

[3] Gibbon's " Autobiography " shows surprisingly little evidence of that vanity for which he was so despised and, even more surprisingly, no trace of recognition of the various members of The Club.

hind their backs men whom he offended to their faces. He purged himself of malice toward some person by speaking out to that person, angrily, scornfully, or insultingly. "He did not hate the persons he treated with roughness, or despise them whom he drove from him by apparent scorn. He really loved and respected many whom he would not suffer to love him." Thus Mrs. Thrale. And Reynolds said that that person who had been bruised in talk by Johnson became therefor the special object of the bruiser's efforts at reconciliation. We are also told that Johnson kept in separate compartments his public and private quarrels, those affecting him as a writer, those as a man, praising in speech the man Macpherson he had called a "ruffian" in writing.

It is possible to be a great writer and a mean man. Johnson's intrinsic greatness lies in that his unguarded moments have not betrayed him. He may have been offensive, but he was not contemptible. The worst we can say of him is that his greatness had limitations. Dozens of persons have recorded his most vagrant comment and they have not diminished him. Few men could have afforded to have made a career of talk; fewer could have survived the test. Except for the Grecian and Latin philosophers and statesmen who taught, enlightened and uplifted by talk, Samuel Johnson is probably the greatest man who chose talk as his chief vocation. Yet he would often regard himself as an idler and promise himself in his Prayers and Meditations to correct this fault. Yet how much more waste was there in the "legitimate" activity of writing as against the supposed illicit activity of talking—as he talked. There is some flaw in the code of morality, writes Robert Lynd in his useful volume on Johnson and his times, "which would commend the literary industry of a Trollope and would condemn the conversational industry of Johnson." Samuel Johnson, in obeying the instinct of his nature, was giving posterity his first fruits. For in talking he was a man using all his powers, whereas, when he sat down to write, he was, by contrast, a maimed man, Mr. Lynd making the felicitous comparison of Johnson the writer with Achilles sulking in his tent, and Johnson the talker with Achilles in battle.

He would talk on matters of which he would not write. He once gravely proved to his "squarson" friend Taylor why a certain recommended bulldog was not commendable and in conversation with a dancing master, so well did he discuss dancing that his vis-à-vis thought Johnson knew more about dancing than he did. He could talk like a sportsman about hunting, although he participated in the sport without enthusiasm. One morning during the Hebridean journey he talked about coining and, that evening, about brewing, in such manner that "Mr. M'Queen said, when he heard the first, he thought he had been bred in the Mint; and when he heard the second, that he had been bred a brewer." Some days later he gave an account of the process of tanning and of the making of whey, among other things, and Boswell discovered, on trying to trap him into a confession of ignorance on some point, that he was familiar even with the details of the butcher's trade. According to Hawkins,

Johnson could not only bind a book, but thatch a cottage. Johnson regretted the decline of prize-fighting because it was an art and no art should be allowed to perish. His prize-fighting uncle, Andrew Johnson, had given him some lessons in self-defense. He talked to soldiers "ostentatiously," as he admitted to Boswell, of the process of granulating gunpowder. He once discussed the possibility of writing a cook book and he possessed apparatus for chemical experiments, of which he was quite fond. He had sufficient scientific curiosity to shave off the hair from his breast and right arm, at the age of seventy, to see if it would grow back again. He sought also to discover how much grapes lost by evaporation. Arkwright declared Johnson was the only person who understood on first view, "the principle and powers" of his most complicated piece of machinery. He was familiar also with "physic," was fond of the company of physicians and even prescribed, as an amateur, in his letters to his old friend Dr. Taylor.

He had the art of extending his knowledge by conversing with all manner of humble per-

OLIVER GOLDSMITH

From a photograph by Emery Walker, after a silhouette ascribed to Ozias Humphry

sons, and enlarged his notions after visiting some iron and copper works in Wales. Addison had remarked to a lady who had complained of his silence: "Madam, I have but ninepence in ready cash but I can draw for a thousand pounds," a remark which fits Goldsmith so well that it has been attributed to him, and Johnson had said of Goldsmith: "As they say of a generous man, it is a pity he is not rich, we may say of Goldsmith, it is a pity he is not knowing. He would not keep his knowledge to himself." But Johnson had all his knowledge in his pocket and did not have to sit with pen before paper in order to draw upon his wealth. At the age of 68 he proudly remarked that there was as little of the old man in his conversation as there was when he was but 28. Remarking on the prevalent habit of talking from books, he said to Boswell, "You and I do not talk from books." The disparity between Johnson the talker and Johnson the writer made even his own generation regard him as the greater man in the former role and look upon Boswell's "Johnson" as greater than almost anything Johnson had ever written. It is even contended that the "Lives of the Poets" is his best work because the Latinity of his writing style is both impregnated and diluted with the vigorous colloquialism of his speech.

CHAPTER EIGHT

"However We May Regret . . ."

HOWEVER we may regret the lack of phonographic records on which might have been engraved and passed down the voice which gave such special force—such bow-wow emphasis—to the statements Johnson made, we do not have occasion to regret the lack of visual representations. The future may have occasion to be grateful—or otherwise—for our bequest to it of George Bernard Shaw in talking movies, should his books be found unsatisfactory. Lacking movies, we have Reynolds's portraits of Johnson, before an engraving of one of which Fanny Burney once heard him call out: "Ah ha! Sam Johnson, I see thee! and an ugly dog thou art!" And we have also the portraits of him which Barry and Humphrys left us. Yet even had the Johnsonian era neglected to bequeath these visual representations to us, its prose—chiefly Boswell's—has done us great service in portraying to us the lineaments, the oddities, the gestures, the manners and mannerisms of the most eccentric Dictator that English letters ever had.

Illness had marked him sufficiently. His scrofula, his melancholy, his St. Vitus's dance, his short-sightedness—these were afflictions sufficient to bow down the back of a man far stronger than Johnson. For a time he lost the sight of one eye and saw but imperfectly with the other. One portrait of Reynolds which called attention to this defect displeased him. (Yet there is another Reynolds's portrait of him in which he is shown with regular, noble features and aspect.[1]) His short-sightedness compelled him to eat fish with his hands for fear of swallowing bones. Ever since his illness in 1766 he suffered from weakness in the knees. He "could not remember the day he had passed free from pain," from his twentieth year. Writing

[1] It is reproduced in this volume facing page 220.

from the Highlands several days after his 64th birthday, he told Mrs. Thrale that he could look back upon a life "diversified by misery, spent part in the sluggishness of penury, and part under the violence of pain, in gloomy discontent or importunate distress." He was in dread of insanity and we recall how like an "ideot" he seemed to Hogarth that day he saw him in the shop of Richardson. And he must have seemed so to others in polite drawing rooms, on those occasions when he was withdrawn and silent. It it no wonder that he did not relish the prospect of resurrection with the same body. And as if his wheezings, puffings and mutterings, his grimaces, contortions and rolling gait, his slovenliness and indifference to clean linen, his dirty hands and bitten nails, the noises betokening satisfaction with his food that he would emit at dinner table—as if these characteristics were not enough to set him apart, he developed a number of superstitious habits which seemed unworthy of his intelligence, even if, like other characteristic habits, they help us to identify him. His caricatural nature makes him the more distinctive a character, not only of literature, but of general biography. It explains, in part, the paradoxical destiny which, in Macaulay's phrase, has befallen Johnson: "To be more intimately known to posterity than other men are known to their contemporaries!"

From his recollection of Johnson in his prime, Boswell gives us this description:

"His figure was large and well formed, and his countenance of the cast of an ancient statue; yet his appearance was rendered strange and somewhat uncouth, by convulsive cramps, by the scars of that distemper which it was once imagined the royal touch could cure, and by a slovenly mode of dress. He had the use only of one eye; yet so much does mind govern and even supply the deficiency of organs, that his visual perceptions, as far as they extended, were uncommonly quick and accurate. So morbid was his temperament, that he never knew the natural joy of a free and vigorous use of his limbs; when he walked, it was like the struggling gait of one in fetters; when he rode he had no command or direction of his horse, but was carried as if in a balloon." Elsewhere Boswell informs us that Johnson's figure had grown "unwieldy from corpulency," that he had become, late in life, "a little dull of hearing." Fanny Burney, describing Johnson as he appeared early in 1777 wrote her correspondent: "He is indeed very ill-favored; is tall and stout but stoops terribly; he is almost bent double. His mouth is almost constantly opening and shutting as if he was chewing. He has a strange method of frequently twirling his fingers and twisting his hands. His body is in continual agitation see-sawing up and down; his feet are never a moment quiet; and in short his whole person is in perpetual motion. He wore "a large wig, snuff-colour coat, and gold buttons, but no ruffles to his shirt . . . and black worsted stockings." His fists are referred to as doughty, but a suspicious erasure leads the editor to believe that the phrase originally was "dirty fists." The following description which Boswell gives of some of Johnson's "singularities" seem to mark rather a witless man than Dr. Johnson.

" . . . while talking or even musing as

he sat in his chair, he commonly held his head to one side towards his right shoulder, and shook it in a tremulous manner, moving the body backwards and forwards, and rubbing his left knee in the same direction, with the palm of his hand. In the intervals of articulating he made various sounds with his mouth, sometimes as if ruminating, or what is called chewing the cud, sometimes giving a half whistle, sometimes making his tongue play backwards from the roof of his mouth, as if clucking like a hen, and sometimes protruding it against his upper gums in front, as if pronouncing quickly under his breath, *too, too, too:* all this accomplished sometimes with a thoughtful look, but more frequently with a smile. Generally when he had concluded a period, in the course of a dispute, by which time he was a good deal exhausted by violence and vociferation, he used to blow out his breath like a Whale. This I suppose was a relief to his lungs; and seemed to him to be a contemptuous mode of expression, as if he had made the arguments of his opponent fly like chaff before the wind." "Pray, Dr. Johnson, why do you make such strange gestures?" a little girl once asked him and he, always tender to children, replied: "From bad habit. Do you, my dear, take care to guard against bad habits."

The habit for which he is perhaps best known was that of touching every post he passed, but he had others as eccentric and for which there was as little reason. He would not, if he could help it, step on the cracks between paving stones; he would break out in the middle of a drawing room conversation with some muttered phrase of the Lord's Prayer. He would put himself to considerable trouble in order to avoid passing a particular alley in Leicester Fields, according to Reynolds's testimony. One habit which he had early contracted was "his anxious care to go out or in at a door or passage by a certain number of steps from a certain point, or at least so that either his right or his left foot, (I am not certain which,) should make the first actual movement when he came close to the door or passage . . . I have, upon innumerable occasions, observed him suddenly stop, and then seem to count his steps with a deep earnestness; and when he had neglected or gone wrong in this sort of magical movement, I have seen him go back again, put himself in a proper posture to begin the ceremony, and, having gone through it, break from his abstraction, walk briskly on, and join his companion." The great Doctor Johnson becomes an idiotic superstitious child. I believe that Mrs. Thrale put her finger on one of the chief causes of his malady when she wrote that "his over-anxious care to retain without blemish the perfect sanity of his mind, contributed much to disturb it." He was known to have twitched off a lady's shoe at a dinner table, on at least one occasion and Langton once saw him absent-mindedly knocking off a porter's load and walking ahead. His fellow-members of The Club observed that after squeezing from the oranges the juice he required for his drink, he would put the rinds in his pocket. Garrick and Beauclerk set Boswell on to find out what he did with the rinds, but he could not find out, beyond observing that they had been nicely scraped and cut into pieces. Reynolds wrote Boswell of one "particularity" of Johnson, namely, that of walking on a floor, step by step, "stretching out his right leg as far as he could reach before him, then bringing up his left leg, and stretching his right still further on," which, observing, his host came up to him and assured him that the flooring was perfectly safe: "The Doctor started from his reverie, like a person waked out of his sleep, but spoke not a word."

Yet despite the various ways in which he seemed to be "touched" in mind and afflicted in body there was something healthily John Bullish in Sam Johnson—in his simple name, the forthrightness of his speech and manner, his Toryism, his morality, his relish in eating, the "gigantick" proportions of his body, the hilarity of his laughter, the conviviality of his habits, even in the drabness of his dress and his slovenliness and in his love of argument. There must have been a core of health in him, however, curious and mad some of his personal peculiarities seem to make him. Long life, hard work, deprivations endured and overcome, these bespeak the presence of that core of health; the relish that he got from life was not a valetudinarian's, and he wasn't always reflecting on his Maker and on his Maker's Hell. During a visit to the Langtons in Lincolnshire, in 1766, he insisted on rolling down a hill, saying he hadn't had a roll in a long time. In Devonshire he had a race with a young woman, kicking off his shoes that he might run the better. He would follow the hounds for fifty miles on end and would deny that he felt either tired or amused. Once when riding on the Brighton Downs, " Single-speech " Hamilton complimented him by saying that he rode for all the world as well as the most illiterate fellow in England. In Paris, during the jaunt with the Thrales, he ran a race in the rain with Baretti. In a race with John Payne, the bookseller who became the chief accountant of the Bank of England, he not only outran that little man, but caught him up, placed him on a tree and continued the " race " alone. The man who could roll, ride and run as Johnson did must have had occasional health in him—health bodily and spiritually. He had courage as well as strength. During a visit to Beauclerk's home in the country he calmly separated two fighting dogs which were frightening the company and he told Boswell that one night he held off four men who had attacked him in the street until the watch came up to relieve him.

There is something in Samuel Johnson of every village tavern king. Something of Sam Johnson peeps out of every cartoon of John Bull. He was John Bullish in his boastfulness, obstinacy, hatred of cant and pretext and meanness and in his respect for the rights of property and title. He is the typical Englishman, a simple man wihout trimmings, without any of the delicacy or finickiness that marks the average "literary" man. And he remains a man's character —whether solemn or gay. Despite his love for the widow Porter who became his wife, his tender thoughtfulness for Mrs. Williams, his fondness for Fanny Burney upon whom he looked as a father and his customary amiability to the other women of the Johnsonian circle, Sam Johnson remains a typical man's character, his name as closely linked to the Mitre Tavern, as is Falstaff's to the Boar's Head. In the tavern he felt no such constraint as he may have borne, at times, in the salon. In nothing was Johnson so John Bullish as in his provincialism, especially in his moral judgments. It was only by Boswell's nagging that he could be persuaded to go into Scotland. He did accompany the Thrales to Wales in the summer of 1774 when his mistress went to take possession of an estate to which she had fallen heir on the death of an uncle. His most frequent visits were to Lichfield, his native city, and Ashbourne, Dr. Taylor's residence, to both of which places he made ten annual excursions in the thirteen-year period, 1767–1779, inclusive, often stopping at Oxford and Birmingham on the way. During his sole jaunt to France—in the company of the Thrales—he was the dyed-in-the-wool Englishman, disdaining to speak French lest the natives have him at a disadvantage. Compare, for example, the contrary conduct of Voltaire during his English stay, with his insatiable curiosity and happy adaptability. Sam Johnson came back to England as he had left it; Voltaire returned to France—to be sure, his stay was for a

GIBBON TAKES SNUFF

A silhouette portrait of the famous historian refreshing himself from his "box"

longer time and he was a younger and more receptive man at the time—an enlarged man. To be sure Johnson knew French, and admitted several authors of that nation into his library, notably Boileau, but what can you expect, he once asked, rhetorically, of people who will eat frogs? Writing to Mrs. Thrale Johnson referred to travel as a futile occupation since towns and countries resemble each other too closely to warrant the inconvenience involved in comparing them. A blade of grass was but a blade of grass wherever it was. "Men and women," he added, "are *my* subjects of inquiry." His own travels, by the way, were for the sake of old friends, not places. "Johnson was not fit to travel," footnotes Baretti, "as every place was equal to him. He mused as much on the road to Paris as he did in his garret in London, as much at a French Opera as in his room in Streatham." He said that he loved to travel in a fast post-chaise with a pretty and intelligent woman as companion, but that was for the sake of the motion. Just before informing us that he himself is a citizen of the world, Boswell stresses Johnson's provincialism, saying that "like the ancient Greeks and Romans, he allowed himself to look upon all nations but his own as barbarians." He referred to the Greeks whom Demosthenes addressed as an assemblage of brutes. Boswell tells us that he has been obliged to humor Johnson in his dislike for Scotchmen as one would humor a child.

The name, character, achievements of Samuel Johnson are little known, if at all, outside English-speaking countries and that is right and that would please him. His provincialism has the reward it sought and desired. In his religious superstitions he did not rise above the class from which he came, if it may be said that he did not sink below it. When told about some skeptical writers of the day, George III expressed the wish that Johnson "would mount his dray-horse and ride over them." He disliked the Scotch and believed in witches and in second sight, prejudices shared by many of the Johnsonian age. He believed in ghosts sufficiently to trouble to look for one. Only John Wesley believed so much more in them that he chided Johnson for not joining in another search for the ghost of Cock Walk. "He was prone to superstition," generalizes Boswell, "but not to credulity." The truth is that Johnson could be judicious and discerning when his religious and moral prejudices were not going to suffer from the scrutiny. His search for truth was conditioned by his prejudices. It has been contended that Johnson did not pursue metaphysical studies for fear that the prejudices in which his mind had found rest might be disturbed. Voltaire called Johnson "a superstitious dog" and was persuaded to change it to "honest fellow" when Boswell told him that Johnson regarded Frederick the Great as Voltaire's literary lackey. Because one, Campbell never passed a church without pulling off his hat, although he had not been in the inside of one for years: "this shows he has good principles." Both Walpole and Cowper derided him in their letters for the old womanishness of his piety, Cowper declaring that he gave evidence of being in religious dotage. Boswell, who had experience of Johnson at his most bullish moments, declared that he had "perhaps at an early period, narrowed his mind somewhat too much, both as to religion and politics," and "that he had many prejudices." According to Baretti, Johnson would have made an excellent Spanish Inquisitor. He declared that only in the contest between persecution and martyrdom could the validity of a new faith be tested; that tolerance was not politic; that none has the right to teach doctrine contrary to that which Society has accepted; that only liberty of conscience is valid.

Although, as a private citizen he sought to save the life of the clergyman-forger Dr. Dodd, writing various petitions, letters and addresses for him, there is on record the report of a conversation in which he declared that were he at the head of the legislature, "I should certainly have signed his death warrant"; he told Hawkins something to the same effect, but whatever his principle, he did, in practice, try to save Dodd's life, although he had never met the man. Harshness to a woman who had married beneath her station was in his code and Boswell's defense of Beauclerk's marriage to a divorced woman genuinely distressed him and he could say: "My dear Sir, never accustom your mind to mingle virtue and vice. The woman's a whore, and there's an end on't." But this did not prevent him from dining with the admired Lady Diana whose drawings Walpole, at least, thought excellent. He believed that the vigorous enforcement of a law passed for the purpose would end prostitution. Carlyle calls him "the last genuine Tory," "the father of all succeeding Tories." To Johnson, above all men, does Carlyle give the credit for saving Britain from the blood-bath of a Revolution, although Lecky, with more justice, gives that credit to Wesley. Johnson and Wesley probably had more in common, spiritually and intellectually, than any two men of that generation not on the infidel side. Violent as Johnson could be, I believe that never, in the whole compass of his life,—except when frothing against the Americans—did he rise to a more apoplectic violence than he did in his "estimate" of Rousseau. "My dear Sir," said Boswell, genuinely distressed, "you don't call Rousseau bad company. Do you really think *him* a bad man?' JOHNSON. 'Sir, if you are talking jestingly of this, I don't talk with you. If you mean to be serious, I think him one of the worst of men; a rascal who ought to be hunted out of society, as he has been. Three or four nations have expelled him; and it is a shame that he is protected in this country." And then after another feeble, and futile, interposition by Boswell on Rousseau's behalf, Johnson continues: "Rousseau, Sir, is a very bad man. I would sooner sign a sentence for his transportation, than that of any felon who has gone from the Old Bailey these many years. Yes, I would like to have him work in the plantations. BOSWELL. 'Sir, do you think him as bad a man as Voltaire?' JOHNSON. 'Why, Sir, it is difficult to settle the proportion of iniquity between them." Boswell remains unpersuaded and confides to his readers that Rousseau's "absurd preference of savage to civilized life, and other singularities, are proofs rather of a defect in his understanding than of any depravity in his heart." Elsewhere he writes: "The beadle within him was often so eager to supply the lash, that the Judge had not time to consider the case with sufficient deliberation." This judgment of Johnson's on Rousseau was anticipated by the French philosopher, but not in all its violence, years before when Boswell had sought him out in his retreat in Switzerland. At the time of Johnson's outburst, Rousseau was in England, having been brought in by David Hume.

As for Voltaire Johnson treated him contemptuously in his Shakespeare preface, although he could say of "Candide" that it had more power than anything else Voltaire had written. He defended the morality and manners of the upper classes and regretted the weakening of the sense of subordination of the lower. He hated the Americans because they owned slaves and scorned the principle of equality. He believed that influence should be in proportion to property. He would have loved to have had a title and sat in Parliament. He became quite angry when Boswell, in a speculative mood, told him that it might have been possible for him, had he pursued another course of life, to have risen to the Lord Chancellorship and to the accompanying rewards and privileges—as angry as if Boswell had surprised an ambition long laid away. Johnson could attempt to dispose of Hume's philosophy by quoting the story of a clergyman in the Bishoprick of Durham.

Even on questions of literary taste he could err as badly. He preferred Richardson to Henry Fielding, calling the latter a blockhead and a barren rascal and quoting, with approbation, Richardson's opinion: " . . . had he not known who Fielding was, he should have believed he was an ostler." Preferring Richardson to Fielding was perhaps a little less heinous a literary offense than preferring Pope's Illiad to Homer's. Apropos of "some ludicrous fantastic dialogues between two coach-horses" which Baretti had published, Johnson said: "Nothing odd will do long. *Tristram Shandy* did not last." To Johnson Swift's work also must have seemed an oddity destined for a short life. He believed that Swift's reputation was better than he deserved and that "The Tale of a Tub" could not be his, for it was too good and the author had not yet acknowledged it. He rated at something below its value "Gulliver's Travels." "Sir, I do not think Gray a first-rate poet . . . His "Elegy in a Churchyard" has a happy selection of images, but I don't like what are called his great things." Asked once to decide the relative status of two poets, Derrick, a minor poet, and Smart, who wrote the lyrical "Song to David," he replied: "Sir, there is no setting the point of precedency between a louse and a flea."[1] He was a Tory in literature as he was in politics: "New sentiments and new images others may produce; but to attempt any further improvements of versification will be dangerous. Art and diligence have now done their best." Enough of Johnson's life has been recorded here to show that those who regarded him as unfit to decide upon the merits of light verse such as Prior's may have had good reason. Cowper asserted that Johnson had not the right to judge of

[1] From another report of this remark it would appear that the comparison was between Derrick and Boyse, which is another matter entirely.

poetry on the subject of love, " a passion which I suppose he never felt in his life," and Walpole, referring to Johnson's dicta on Gray, Swift and Fielding, as well as on Prior, likens him to an elephant who, having become literate, should decide that " an Arabian horse is a very clumsy ungraceful animal. Pass to a better chapter!" Yet Walpole himself was not infallible in his judgments, to him "Tristram Shandy" was "the dregs of nonsense" and he over-rated Gray beyond his desserts: who indeed can judge correctly of *all* one's contemporaries?

Although Reynolds was one of his dearest friends, the art he practiced meant nothing to Johnson. He could sit in a room the walls of which were crowded with masterpieces " and never feel the slightest disposition to turn them, if their backs were outermost." He could rate painting as an inferior art than literature on the purely moral ground that " painting, Sir, can illustrate, but cannot inform." In the same utilitarian spirit he dismissed ornamental architecture and ridiculed statuary. How John Bullish that is! One of his objections to Fielding was that he drew pictures of low life, although he did not contest the assertion, which Boswell made, that the pictures he drew were natural. Music meant little, if anything, to him. It is true that he bought himself a "flagelet" and attended some of Dr. Burney's famous musicales but "I never made out a tune" and he could not sympathize with Boswell's sometimes tearful sensibility to music. (In his youth Boswell had played the German flute and painted at least one water-color.) "And pray, Sir, who is Bach?" he asked Dr. Burney. "Is he a piper?" The extent of his musical knowledge may be derived from the fact that he could tell the difference between a drum and a trumpet, and a bagpipe and a guitar. There is one Johnsonian judgment which survives rather because of the felicity of its expression than of its truth. When Hannah More expressed her disappointment with the sonnets of the author of "Paradise Lost," Johnson answered: "Milton, Madam, was a genius that could cut a Colossus from a rock; but could not carve heads upon cherry-stones." In another felicitious remark he compared Corneille to a clipped hedge and Shakespeare to a forest.

Yet these errors, too, these limitations, like his physical mannerisms, do help to endear the man to us, after they have helped us to an easy and convenient identification. There are no subtleties in the man. We love him for the forthrightness of manner which enabled him to speak out the thing that was on the surface of his mind, instead of attempting, with that desire for "fairness" which seems to be the blight of neuter critics, to smother his true opinion. He lived in a sturdy time, when authors were expected to take blows and survive them. He could read a "ludicrous imitation" of his style in a review and show how it might have been bettered. Johnson was the representative of a time in which reviews did not kill sensitive poets. "I would rather be attacked than unnoticed," he said. Referring to a neglected philologist who had run from the world he declared for this principle of conduct; "I hate a fellow whom pride, or cowardice, or laziness drives into a corner, and does nothing when he is there but sit and *growl;* let him come out, as I do, and *bark*." There was no bitterness, malice, or envy in that bark. We treasure Samuel Johnson because he is an individual. We may have outgrown his social and religious prejudices. Time may have proved him wrong north, west, south and east and in-between points of the compass. All his books, except possibly The Lives of the Poets, may serve only as dust-gatherers, but these things make him none the less a man who endeared himself to his time and who, through Boswell, has endeared himself to posterity. We possess Samuel Johnson by the gracious and patient gift of James Boswell, whose life was merged in that of his master and whose reputation derives from his master and yet gives it its glory. We are sure of the innate greatness of Samuel Johnson, since not even the patient notations of a Boswell have diminished his proportions. Most heroes cannot be heroic all the time. We see Johnson under every light and every shade, and with all his blemishes upon him we accept him, love him, pity him and understand him, however we may differ with him. For he was a genuine man, even if he was not a composite of all the desirable graces and even if he did not successfully anticipate the views of this generation. Johnson had the strength of his convictions. It is easy to be wise with the negative wisdom which intervening generations have stored up for us. We call the articles of his creed prejudices, but hold our own convictions far more lightly—hold them, assuming we have any. He would not be tolerant for he could not afford to be indifferent about things that mattered. He was a Christian moralist, not a pagan philosopher. We must accept him within the limitations in which he himself gloried. Like Gibbon, we can afford to be superior, but we can also harbor a lurking envy of a creed so simple that it was possible to have faith in it. Sam Johnson was the last representative of the age of faith.

Bibliographical Postscript

I have read and re-read, perused and dipped into more than sixty volumes over a period of three years in the preparation of this work. It would be a futile parade of industry to list all the sources examined and consulted. Among those volumes, however, were some which no previous commentator or essayist had had the opportunity to read, namely, the first six volumes of the privately printed Boswell Papers. I take this opportunity to thank Harry Hansen, my colleague on The World; William Soskin, of The New York Evening Post, and William Edwin Rudge for their kindness in permitting me to examine copies of these volumes in their possession, or custody. But my deepest sense of gratitude is reserved for E. Byrne Hackett of the Brick Row Book Shop, and not only for the loan of valuable books; and for the gentlemen of the New York branch of the Oxford University Press for permission to read other source books which I could not buy.

September, 1929 H. S.

FINIS

Special title page, and front matter design of this book are by Richard W. Ellis of the Georgian Press, Westport, Conn.